Making A Ripple
The 2x4 Canoe

Copyright © 2015

All rights reserved.

No part of this book may be reproduced in any form or by any electronic or mechanical means including information storage and retrieval systems, without permission in writing from the author. The only exception is by a reviewer, who may quote short excerpts in a review.

ISBN 978-1507734193

Printed in the United States of America

Published by: BackWood Basics Press

www.backwoodbasics.com

01012015   Book Design by Design Angler, Inc., Bemidji MN

The author of this book cannot guarantee that creating and using the products described in this book are safe for everyone. This book is therefore sold without warranties or guarantees of any kind, expressed or implied, and the author disclaims any liability for any resultant injuries, losses, or damages of any kind.

Dedication

This book is dedicated to the memory of my father, Rudy Schultz, whose skilled hands were guided by both patience and perseverance. With every passing year that I grow a bit wiser I am more proud and grateful to be his son.

Introduction

Every weekend, during the ice-free months in our northern Minnesota community of Turtle River, we are entertained by a steady parade of large fishing boats being pulled behind necessarily large pick-up trucks, as their owners come up US highway 71 seeking some of the world's best walleye waters. Most of these rigs have already been traveling over 200 miles as the Twin Cities empty of their work-weary adventurers on Friday afternoons; folks who have invested heavily in the equipment that they feel is necessary for them to escape the urban madness for a few days. As they pass me, I cannot help but tally-up the cost of the boat, trailer and towing vehicle, and generally arrive at a figure of $60,000 to $80,000. While, as a fisherman, I should be plagued with envy, I just get tired thinking of the long hours of work, the hours spent in heavy traffic, and the stress of taking on big payments (only to find that your buddy has a new rig that is even bigger), just to spend a few precious hours on the lake.

Fishing boats, of course, have their place, and we would not be without one; ours, however, is a reclaimed hull that was rescued from the land-fill, and has less value than the sonar equipment on the glitter boats. My idea of a relaxation-response to the hectic pace of our mechanized life is to head for a little secluded lake in a small craft; one that could not get onto that lake if it was any bigger or heavier. The choices for such a small craft are many, if one is made of money, or has a willingness to take on more debt. For me, however, a big part of the relaxation comes from knowing that my craft, while safe, stable and attractive, was made for very little money or time. By very little I mean about $300 and about 30-40 hours. In pursuit of such a craft, I have created Ripple.

Ripple is a 14' canoe with a 36" beam that is best described as a hybrid. Ripple is not a flat-sided, flat-bottomed plywood canoe, nor is she a round-bottomed cedar stripped craft; she is comfortably nestled in-between these 2 extremes in the world of wooden canoe construction.

After building a 12' plywood solo canoe from purchased plans, I was impressed by the ease of construction of this craft, using just 2 sheets of plywood, but was disappointed when the end result had too little free-board and an unsettlingly narrow beam. It was hoped that my son, Conor, and I would each build one of these canoes, so that we could venture into the Boundary Waters Canoe Area Wilderness (BWCAW); each in our own light-weight solo craft. Since he was much smaller than I was at the time, I figured this first attempt would become his canoe, but for myself I felt that I required a more substantial craft. I therefore purchased a second set of plans and built a 14 footer, which was longer, but, due to the size constraints imposed by 2 sheets of plywood, was still too narrow and too close to the waterline to be loaded with gear and taken into the Boundary Waters. I was, at the time, about 30 pounds heavier than I am today, and feared that I looked a bit too much like an elephant sitting on a water ski in this tiny craft. These 2 canoes became fun toys for us (without gear) to take out on the lake on calm days, but one became too intimate with the water surface to use them for serious fishing, or for over-night canoe-camping. Their use was also restricted to the warm weather months (or weeks here in northern Minnesota), since sitting on the floor inevitably meant sitting in a puddle of water, as the double paddle trickled water into the canoe with each stroke.

I wanted a canoe that was 14 feet in length, since we could then carry it inside of our enclosed cargo trailer, which doubles as a camping trailer. I wanted a canoe with more freeboard and beam than 2 sheets of plywood could offer, and I wanted the option of carrying 2 people and a loaded pack. Going to 3 sheets of plywood would allow me to build a larger canoe, but, at $110 for a sheet of 4mm Okoume (an African hardwood used to make the best marine plywood), a plywood canoe was becoming either too expensive, or, if I went with less expensive plywood, too heavy. A cedar strip canoe, the ones that folks spend hundreds of hours on- meticulously applying milled strips to create the equivalent of a piece of fine furniture- was out of my time, temperament and price range. I wanted a quick and easy compromise; a canoe that was a step above a stitch and tape plywood one, and a few steps below a two thousand dollar thing of beauty that I would not dare to put into the water.

Northern Minnesota is blessed with more than its share of small lakes that are full of fish; but they are not accessed by roads, and therefore do not allow folks with boats on trailers access to these waters. The idea was to create a craft that one could pull on a trailer behind a bicycle- or even by hand- to access these tranquil, productive, secluded waters and enjoy a day of solitude. To do so requires a canoe of reasonably lightweight construction, but also one with enough stability to enjoy a day of fishing without worrying about sneezing and having the canoe unexpectedly capsize, along with lots of expensive fishing gear.

I chose northern white cedar as the building material for my prototype because I enjoy working with cedar; it is decay resistant, bends and sands easily, is light, strong, attractive, and is locally available at a reasonable cost. The main thing I do not like about using cedar is the fact that it has, due to our infestation of whitetail deer, pretty much become a non-renewable tree species. Deer will browse every single cedar seedling that tries to grow, leaving our cedar swamps devoid of regeneration. I tried, however, to rationalize the use of white cedar by telling myself that I would simply work harder to thin the deer herd. Once I had decided on my building material, I just needed a design. So I drew one up, cut-out a ¼ scale set of forms, and bent thin cedar strips around them to construct a quarter- sized canoe. The model turned out pretty good, but the bottom was too flat, and there was no rocker; in other words, it was a bit too easy to build. I therefore added some rocker, and put a shallow V down the keel. Unfortunately I did not re-draw the plans with these changes and build a new ¼ scale model incorporating them; I made the changes during the construction of the full-sized prototype. This seat-of-the-pants method of canoe design would make any marine architect shudder, as I changed my form dimensions several times while I wrestled with a bottom panel that I had pre-cut and fiber-glassed together as one football-shaped unit back when I thought I was making a flat-bottomed canoe. As a result, the construction of my first canoe was not as straight-forward as it had been in my mind while designing it in my head during those early morning hours before getting out of bed. The pre-fabricated bottom was screwed on and taken off several times, as I shaved down both the forms and the bottom panel to get close to my desired configurations. Since the sides and the now-modified bottom no longer matched, I ended up with some creative gap filling on my prototype. Having made so many changes to the forms during the construction process, I relegated them to the burn pile after building the prototype and made a whole new set- incorporating my new dimensions- for my second canoe.

This time, however, I built another scale model before building the real thing; to be sure this was to indeed be the final design.

The eventual result was all that I had hoped it would be. She is not a round bottomed, brightly varnished, flawless work of art; nor is she a flat-sided, flat- bottomed bookcase shaped plywood canoe. Ripple is, as I said, a hybrid. Her slight V, and generous rocker, makes her a lively performer, although her wide, fairly flat bottom keeps her from becoming a temperamental speedster looking to throw her rider at any moment (I threw the her references in there because that's what we are supposed to do when referring to a vessel-it had nothing to do with the comment about a wide, fairly flat bottom). Once finished, it is hard to believe that this is a craft that can be constructed from four 16' 2x4s. After the forms are cut and assembled on a platform, the hull can easily be formed in a weekend. This is a fun craft to build, and one that the builder can be proud to say "I made it myself." Besides sharing my design, I want to share some building tricks that I learned along the way. These short-cuts not only help to stream-line the building process, but they also help the builder save a considerable amount of money on materials, which, if your book-keeper is anything like mine, will be greatly appreciated.

What's in a Name?

I realized that my canoe design needed a name, just as a car needs a name, to define the model. A book titled "Building a 14' Canoe" just did not seem to be a sound marketing strategy. With the hundreds of canoe designs out there, I figured that most of the good names (but not the good designs) were taken, but I wanted one that best defined the character and intended purpose of this canoe. A name like Whitewater or Chasm Chaser, for example, just did not define the character of my canoe; I wanted a name that brought to mind a glass-calm small lake with nobody on it but me, slowly dipping a paddle while dragging a floating Rapala and creating scarcely a ripple. Ripple! I had my name. The name evokes just the image that I was searching for. If there are other canoe designs out there with the same name, I am unaware of them, and I did not steal this name from anyone-honest. This does not mean, of course, that anyone who builds this canoe must use that name. If you are like me, you do not assign a name to a small watercraft. I know my fishing buddies would snicker (or worse) if I had a name emblazoned across the transom of our fishing boat. "Say Dave, Miss Louise and I are heading out walleye fishing; want to come along?" You get the picture. To identify our canoes I usually say something like: "Do you want the red one or the green one?"

Equipment List

Probably the scariest piece of equipment on this list, for some, is the planer. Not having one does not mean that you cannot build this canoe; it only means that you will have to find someone to plane some planks for you. The raw material used to build this canoe is 2x4 framing lumber which means that the planks must first be ripped on a table saw and then finished by running them through a planer. There really is no way around this, but any wood shop can perform this task for you for a fee, which may be enough incentive for you to purchase a planer. Planers today are not necessarily the massive thousand pound machines that we grew up using in high school wood shop; they are small, portable, fairly inexpensive, amazingly good performers that are fun to use. Once purchased, it tends to be one of those pieces of equipment that we wonder how we ever did without it. The only other big piece of necessary equipment is a table saw, and since a table saw is generally the first big piece of equipment that a woodworker will purchase, I will assume that you own one, or have a friend who owns one. So here is the list:

Table saw, planer, miter saw, random orbital sander, belt sander, saber saw, Japanese saw, circular saw (preferably a small, cordless one), one or two drills (preferably cordless), packing tape dispenser, 12" taping knife, scissors (cheap ones that can be thrown out), hot glue gun, heat gun, lots of spring clamps and C-clamps, and a leaf blower (or at least a shop vacuum).

Supplies

Besides the equipment, supplies will include: Four 16' red cedar 2x4s, One sheet of ¾" particle board (plus another partial sheet), 3 or four 8' 2x4s, two pounds of #6 drywall screws, clear packing tape, masking tape, tongue depressors (more appropriately known as craft sticks), containers for mixing and measuring epoxy resin and putty, about 1 quart of type 1 water-proof wood glue, wood flour (sanding dust), 1 and 1/2 gallons of epoxy resin, blended filler (a mixture of micro-balloons and colloidal silica), 24 ounces of epoxy fairing compound, a roll of 3" fiberglass tape, 5 yards of 50" wide 12 ounce bi-axial fiberglass fabric, 5 yards of 30" wide 4 ounce fiberglass cloth, small box of 16 gauge paneling (ring) nails, coarse and medium sanding discs, dust mask, paint and primer, a 4" mini roller along with 4-6 mini foam roller pads, micro-fiber cloth, and a bit of thin wire. Whatever material you choose to build a platform for the forms will also be required; I made two 2x4 frames covered with 1/2" oriented strand board (2 sheets), for my platform.

We will discuss the use of these materials in exhaustive detail as we go through each step of the building process. The list is thrown out here now to weed-out the faint of heart, and have them donating this book to a local used book sale fund raiser. Actually, it is not anywhere near as daunting as it appears, and is much less complicated than most boat building projects, in my experience. So let's get started.

Strips vs. Planks

When I built my prototype using white cedar I made the mistake of calling the construction material strips, whenever I described my project to anyone who would listen to me. Hearing cedar strip canoe, however, conjures up images of a fine-furniture quality watercraft. Upon seeing my canoe, with its hard chine, wide boards and painted exterior, it was apparent that they were not seeing several months (or years) of meticulous labor to create a work of art. I was not embarrassed or ashamed of my canoe- on the contrary, I am quite pleased with this design- but to avoid misleading folks I decided to call my strips planks. So, although the word plank tends to bring to mind the construction material for a Spanish galleon, I will let the canoe snobs have their strips.

The Lumber

As previously mentioned, I built my prototype using white cedar, thinking that, since strip canoes are made from cedar, mine must be too. White cedar is a wonderful wood to use and results in a beautiful, lightweight, decay-resistant canoe. Living in northern Minnesota I have access to some small mills that buy white cedar stumpage from private landowners. Since white cedar is, as mentioned, non-renewable in northern Minnesota now that deer have replaced the native moose, elk and woodland caribou, the removal of cedar is not generally allowed on State and Federal lands. White cedar is also difficult to mill, since larger logs tend to be hollow, and frequent knots generally do not allow for the creation of long, clear boards. Cedar planks must therefore be scarf-joined together to create the necessary lengths. White cedar is also usually sold rough-cut, meaning the lumber must first be planed to a uniform thickness prior to ripping it into planks.

None of this is very difficult, but the purpose of this book is to offer plans and instructions for a canoe that is easily and inexpensively constructed using locally available materials. An alternative to using white cedar is to purchase dimensional red cedar (actually juniper) lumber from a building supply store. One can generally find 16' long red cedar 2x4s that are both straight and fairly knot-free. I decided, however, to really make the purists shudder and built a canoe from some off-the-rack 16' 2x4 pine framing lumber. I could see no reason why this would not work, which is why I build prototypes before going off peddling my latest idea. I bought 4 fairly clear 2x4s, ripped them into 16' long planks and finished them in the planer. I was pleased to create enough full-length planks to form the hull with no scarf joints. My pleasure ended, however, when I attempted to set my first plank along the shear, because, unlike the more cooperative cedar, the pine stubbornly resisted being bent in the 2 directions that it must do to define the shear of the canoe. The flat side of the plank would easily bend into a U shape, but my efforts to get the thin edge to simultaneously arc along the shear left me with bulges, twists and dips between the forms. I persevered, however, and eventually coaxed the planks to lie reasonably true along the shear. I did this by drilling a pilot hole, screwing the plank to one stem, bending the plank forcefully up and over a temporary screw at the shear line on the middle form, and forcefully working the plank down to the other stem, where I attached it with a screw. I then put a screw through the plank at the center form, and worked, form by form, to one stem, and then the other. It was a bugger, and I will not likely use pine 2x4s again. I had similar bulging problems along the chine, but those I minimized by backing off the screws a bit to relieve some of the tension prior to installing the bottom. After installing both sides I was very close to unscrewing the whole works from the forms and hauling it to the burn pile, before putting more time and materials into this canoe; cutting my losses, so to speak. I decided to see it through, however; partly out of curiosity, and partly to prove that a canoe can be built from lowly framing lumber if one is willing to put up with its bad behavior.

So, not wanting to subject anyone who buys this book to a struggle with uncooperative planks, the wood of choice became Western red cedar 2x4s from the building supply store. Selecting the right 2x4s for the project may take some planning and a store clerk with a sense of humor. When selecting our lumber, we must remember that it is not intended for canoe construction; it is intended for deck construction, and for other home building projects. But somewhere in that pile there may be four 2x4s that are fairly knot-free, dry and straight. If the selection is poor, you may have to go elsewhere, or await another shipment. It also may require some opportunistic shopping; if a clear and straight 2x4 is spotted on one trip, it may be prudent to buy it and store it for the eventual project. Here in Bemidji, I have the option of purchasing either finished 2x4s, which are actually 3 and 1/2"x 1 and 1/2", with a radius cut on the finished edges, or rough-cut 2x4s, which are 3 and 7/8"x 1 and 7/8". The finished lumber is slightly cheaper, but one can get more, and wider, planks from the rough-cut lumber. The lumber of choice, I believe, is the rough-cut Western red cedar. With planks that have a finished width of 1 and 3/4", one can plank a side with 7 full planks, and use only 27 full-length planks (16') to build the hull.

Creating Planks from 2x4s

Ripping 16' 2x4 lumber into ¼" thick planks takes some planning. First, one needs some wide-open spaces. It also requires at least 2 roller stands, a feather-board is very (very) helpful, and a good quality table saw (which I do not have) with a good sharp ripping blade helps, too. If the wood is carefully selected there should be no need for scarf joints. If using rough-cut 2x4s the faces will need to be planed prior to ripping them into planks; both for a uniform width and since this will become the plank edge which will become a glue joint. If using finished 2x4s, set the rip fence so that the first planks off the board are thick enough so that the plane will remove all signs of the radius and still leave enough for a square edged 1/4" finished plank. Remember to repeat the procedure for each of the boards before moving the rip fence; we want each of our planks to be as uniform as possible. Then set the rip fence to rip 5/16" planks, with the help of the feather board, which is made from plastic and mounts on a track that fits inside the miter gauge slot on the table saw. Perhaps folks with a fancy and powerful table saw can set the fence to cut a 5/16" plank, and run all the boards through at that setting, but my nearly 30 year old table saw is not up to the task. I must take off the 5/16" from each board, and then slide the fence 7/16" closer to the blade, repeating this until all of the boards have been ripped into planks. This is not ideal, but, until I can afford a powerful new saw, this is how I have to do it. Moving the fence 7/16" closer to the blade will leave a 5/16" rough plank, after subtracting for the blade width. The measurement is made between the rip fence and an inward leaning saw tooth. Remember to run all of the boards through before re-setting the rip fence; the feather board should need no re- adjustment. A feather board, though not essential for ripping planks, is certainly worth the $15 investment to hold the boards firmly against the rip fence; both to reduce the wavering of the cut and for added safety. Even when using stands on each end of the saw (2 on each end would be even better), these long boards are unwieldy; especially when working alone, which I almost always do.

Once the boards have been turned into rough planks, we need to use the planer to turn them all into planks of a uniform, smooth 1/4" thickness. First we need to take down the thicker planks that have the radius, if using finished 2x4s. Then we can add them to the stack of planks waiting to be finished. Since there are bound to be some broken plank segments due to knots, it is best to use one of these broken pieces to check the planer depth. We are looking to remove only about 1/32" from the first face. Once satisfied with the planer depth setting, run all of the planks through the planer, again using the roller stands to support them. Fortunately at least 4 planks can be run through the planer at a time, so this goes fairly quickly, and is actually quite fun, in my opinion. There is something pleasing about seeing the transformation from framing lumber into fine-quality thin planks. As the planks are run through the planer, set them aside with all of the planed faces in the same direction. Once all of the planks have had one face planed, adjust the planer for a finished plank that is 1/4" thick. Verify the thickness with the scrap piece, and run all of the planks through the planer to finish the other face. The entire process of turning rough-cut 2x4s into enough finished planks to build the canoe takes me about 2 hours, and produces an impressive pile of saw dust.

If the boards were fairly clear of knots, there should be enough full-length planks to cover the canoe without having to make any scarf joints. Each side of the canoe will use 7 or 8 full-length planks, depending on whether finished or rough-cut 2x4s have been selected. The bottom will require two 13 and 1/2 footers, two 12 and 1/2 footers, two 11 and 1/2 footers, two 10 and 1/2 footers, two 9 and 1/2 footers, two 8 footers, two 7 footers, two 5 and 1/2 footers, and, if using 1 and 3/4" planks, a 3 footer ripped length-wise to cover a small remaining gap.

Plank Splicing-The Scarf Joint

For those who prefer to use white cedar to fabricate their planks, I am including the method that I use to create scarf joints. This is not necessarily a recommended method, but it worked for me, and I survived the experience with all of my appendages and vision; safety cannot be over-stressed for this method.

Using the miter saw, clamp a piece of 2x6 onto the deck and cut a thin piece from it to create a square fence for the plank. Next, set the blade at 5 degrees (away from the wood) and, using a stand to support its length, set the plank against the 2x6 edge. Then, with fingers well back from the saw blade, slowly lower the blade to cut a wedge of wood from the plank. If the cut is made too quickly the saw tends to pull on the plank and skew the cut. Be aware that the wedge, once freed, may become a projectile. Serious eye protection is a must.

After all of the plank sections to be joined have been beveled, apply a good coat of waterproof glue to one face, align the joint, and cover one side of the joint with about a 12" piece of packing tape. The tape not only temporarily holds the sections together, but also prevents them from being glued to each other when several joints are stacked inside of the clamps.

Be sure that the joint is straight, and that the sections lap as they should, so that the plank in the joint area is the same thickness as the rest of the plank. Set several (up to 11) taped-together joints on a plastic-covered flat floor and clamp them up with at least two C-clamps. This creates a strong joint; my attempts to break it have resulted in the plank breaking well outside of the joint.

Also, after sanding, this joint is nearly invisible. It may be necessary to create a few scarf joints if the wood being used was plagued by too many knots. If one thinks of it as a splice, the process seems a bit less daunting; just a quick and easy way to cut-out a knot and re-join the segments to create a complete plank.

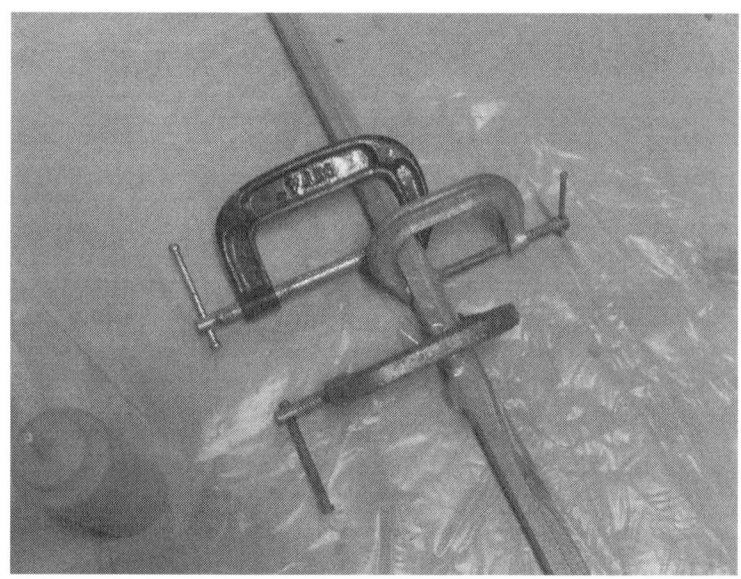

First the Forms

Once the full-length planks have been created, the next step is to bend them around the forms, which we need to build. If there is any groaning after reading the previous sentence, let me assure you that it is not difficult, nor expensive or time consuming, to draw, cut-out, and set-up a set of forms upon which you will construct this canoe. I use ¾" particle board for my forms because it is relatively cheap, it resists warping (as long as it is kept dry), and is easy to cut and shape. The disadvantages include its weight- the stuff is very heavy and unwieldy- and the fact that it is just glued-together saw dust which tends to crumble and split when screws are driven into its edge, giving it a fairly short useful life as a form. For two canoes it is fine. For 3 or 4 canoes, it is also OK, but I would dress the edges with some slightly thickened wood glue to fill the screw holes and repair chips and splits between uses. I searched the clearance bins, where damaged panels are marked-down due to broken edges or corners, and found enough to make all of my forms for about $13. A broken-off corner can easily be worked around when laying out the forms. **Ripple's form diagrams are included at the end of this book.**

Lay out each of the forms on the particle board using the supplied dimensions, remembering that 2 of each must be made, except for the biggest one (#6), which goes in the center. Only one of each must be drawn, however, since, once cut-out, it becomes a template for the other matching form. Using a saber saw, cut out the forms by doing your best to keep the cut on the outside of the pencil line. For this process it is well worth the extra buck or 2 to purchase the hollow-cut saber saw blades made for a fine, precision cut. The shape can then be brought down to its lines easily with the belt or orbital sander. Once the material is cut inside of the line, however, there is no bringing the material back.

Cut some 2x4s slightly shorter than the forms, and attach them flush with the form bottoms to serve as a base that will be attached to a platform (called a strongback in boat-building terms). Be sure that the centerline is marked on the form side opposite the 2x4, so that it can be centered along the centerline on the platform. Before screwing the 2x4s to the form, I run the edge that will be up against the form through the table saw to remove the radius and give it a nice square, flat face. I built a base out of 2x4s covered with ½" oriented strand board (OSB) that was a couple of inches shorter than the total canoe length, so that the stem end of the forms extends beyond the base. The 44" x 82" bases I made are then screwed together, and set-up on concrete blocks. This makes a nice base for the forms, since it creates a shelf along both sides of the canoe; both for working from, and for catching epoxy drips. It is also handy for storage between canoe projects. Simply remove the center form (#6), remove the screws holding the 2 halves of the base together, and the 2 sections can then be stacked against a wall, along with the attached forms. This canoe is so simple (and fun) to build that you may end up building more than one of

them. Or the forms can be passed-on to another aspiring canoe builder.

There are 3 essential things to remember when attaching the forms to a base. First, draw a centerline and have all of the forms centered on it, and on the perpendicular station lines. Second, be sure that the end of the stem form extends past the base. Third, work on a flat floor, or have the platform leveled if the floor is not. Whatever you decide to use as a base upon which to attach the forms, it should be set up on blocks or legs to create a comfortable work height. The forms should then be squared to the base, using braces if necessary to keep the forms plumb (straight up and down).

Planking the Canoe (Finally)

Once the forms are secured to the base, all of the edges of the forms are covered with packing tape to prevent the glue from sticking to them. The shear must be marked on each side of the center form (#6), and be visible through the packing tape. The first plank to be installed will be flush with the stem top (floor side) at the ends, and at the shear-line on the center form. It is a bit tricky- but very important- to get this first plank installed correctly, since all subsequent planks will follow the contour of this first plank.

I suppose having 2 people at this point is the best way to install the first plank, but that takes the fun out it. So I start by screwing a temporary 3" wood screw into the center form just below the shear-line to hold the plank up as I drill a pilot hole and then screw one end of the plank into the stem form, flush with its top (floor side). Then I bend the plank, as tightly as possible against the forms, over the temporary screw, down to the tip of the other stem, and fasten it (temporarily) with a wood screw after drilling a pilot hole. Next, I drill a pilot hole close to the bottom edge of the plank (this is why 2 drills are recommended- one has a drill bit and the other has a driver bit), and put one wood screw into the plank on the center form, to draw the wood tightly to the form. Then drill pilot holes through the plank- near the bottom edge where it wants to bulge out from the form- at the #5 forms on each side of the center form. Drill a pilot hole, and insert a screw at the #4 forms, again drawing the bottom edge to the form. If there is some bulging of the plank toward the stems at this point, remove the stem screw to relieve the pressure, insert screws in the remaining forms (#3 and #2), and re-insert the stem screw last.

Working in this manner toward the stems, I get a well-laid first plank that follows the sweep of the shear without bulges or dips that could result from starting at one end or the other, or starting in the center and working towards one stem, and then the other. This sounds complicated and confusing, and is difficult to explain, but don't worry, it will likely explain itself as you go through the process of installing the first plank. The main point is to have the first plank lay naturally against the forms from the shear mark on the center form down to the tip of each stem. The photos showing the process should help to de-mystify it. Note that 2 screws are put through the plank at each form. Since we use wide planks, one screw would not pull it snugly against the form at each edge; especially on the rounded portions. Just snug the screws up so that the plank is against the form, and do not over-tighten or counter-sink the screw into the wood, since it splits easily; especially the red cedar.

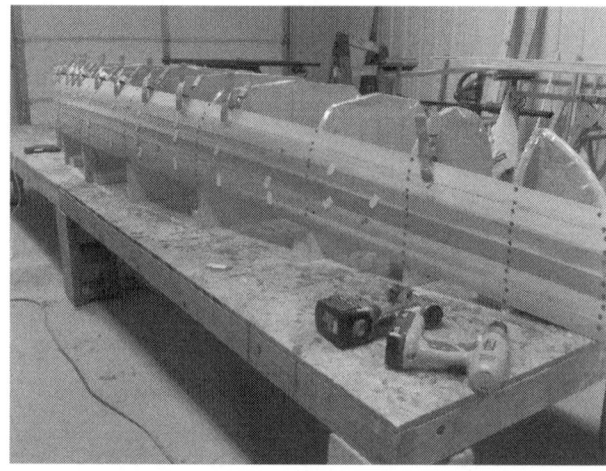

Once the first plank is in place, the rest of them go on quickly and easily (until the last one). I like to start at the stem and work, form by form, to the other stem. There are two important considerations to keep in mind as one installs the planks, which greatly reduces the amount of sanding down the road:

First, take the time to align the planks so that they seat flush on top of each other. The plank being installed on top should be right on top of the plank below it, without any displacement. This is not difficult to do, but it does take some

persuasion in some spots to assure proper plank alignment prior to screwing them down to the forms. Usually the plank seats nicely right on top of the one below it, without any complaints. If there is some stubborn displacement after the screws are installed, a bit of hot glue on a 1" piece of tongue depressor (craft stick) pressed across the joint should hold the 2 planks flush. Do not, however, try to hold the hot wood piece in place until the glue hardens. Not only is it hot on the fingers, but it takes a few minutes for the hot glue to harden sufficiently to hold the joint together. Place the hot glued stick piece over the joint, and then clamp it using a spring clamp. By the time you start the next plank the clamps can be removed. To remove the pieces of hot-glued wood once it is time to do so, simply heat them with a heat-gun and scrape them off with a putty knife or wood chisel. Sometimes a piece of packing tape will do the trick, or, for a real stubborn section, a stitch or 2 using some thin wire may be needed to pull the 2 planks into alignment. I built the non-compliant pine 2x4 canoe, however, using only hot glued craft stick pieces and some packing tape, so I would not worry too much about the need for wire. The hot-glued stick pieces should not be placed in the center, between the forms, because this is where the fiberglass tape will be applied to strap the hull together. This will be discussed in more detail later, but this area will be sanded to its finished shape before gluing down the tape, so the craft stick pieces need to be installed on either side of the mid-sections between forms.

Second, try not to use so much glue on the plank edge that it oozes-out and hardens on the inside of the canoe. The glue, when dry, is not much fun to sand off. I fill a mustard squeeze bottle (the kind with the long, tapered nozzle) with wood glue to apply a thin bead of glue to the plank edge. Although I have not tried it, I suspect that a ketchup bottle would work equally well.

The glue is not structural; it is just necessary to temporarily hold the planks together once the screws are removed from the forms. Once sheathed with 12 ounce fiberglass cloth, the glue is no longer needed to hold the planks together. So use enough, but not too much, glue.

Continue laying up the planks until the last full strip extends past the chine (the angle where the side meets the bottom) on the forms. At this point, begin at each stem and attach shorter planks until all of the side planks extend above the chine. The plank segments that extend only partway toward the center from the stems can be secured to the plank below it using tape or hot-glued stick pieces-both on the inside and on the outside- until the glue dries. The final plank segment may need some trimming, using a utility knife or wood chisel, to get the portion toward the center of the canoe to lie flat against the plank below it. This may be one area that a bit of stitching with wire may be in order.

The final full-length plank can be difficult to get to conform to the rounded forms. As with all of the planks, they should be forced against both the form and the plank below it to get it to lie true and create a strong glue joint between the planks. Even with lots of persuasion, however, this top plank tends to bulge out between the forms as it is screwed into place; although this is mostly resolved once the screws are backed-out a bit. In fact, to cut the excess wood (once the glue dries), the screws in the path of the saw are all removed, and the planks should pull away from the forms enough to eliminate the bulges.

Once the planks are all installed on the first side of the canoe, the overhanging wood must be trimmed from the stems before the planks can be installed on the other side of the canoe. To trim the stems, cover the tape-covered stem form with a piece of 3/8" flexible tubing , both to prevent the tape from being cut into by the saw, and to extend the line of the stem out a bit from the form so the gap can be filled with thickened epoxy. Use the Japanese saw, set lightly against the tubing, to trim the wood from the stems. I find that it works best to begin cutting up from the floor side. The second canoe side can now be installed, and the excess wood from the second side can be trimmed from the stems using the trimmed first side as a guide, without the need for the tubing. Covering both sides with planks should take 3-4 hours.

Once the glue has dried on both sides of the canoe, usually over-night, the excess wood must be trimmed from the side/bottom joint (chine). The best method I have found to do this is to tack a paneling (or finishing) nail part-way into the wood at the side/bottom joint on each of the forms-with the nail set perpendicular to the plank at each station. Then temporarily install a 15' long batten on the underside of the nails by tacking it in place with paneling nails on each end, and use a pencil to draw the sweep of the arc that defines the side/ bottom joint. The batten to be used for this arc can be cut from a spare full-length plank, but, to bend freely, should be only about ½" wide. Once the pencil line is drawn, the batten, nails, and any screws in the way of the blade are removed, and, using a small circular saw with the blade depth set to cut only through the plank (and not into the packing tape covering the forms), carefully make a cut along the length of the pencil line. Repeat the process on the other side of the canoe. Then sand the cut edge to create a uniform line that nicely follows the curve of the chine, and continues the bottom angle found at each of the forms. A small piece of board may be laid over pairs of forms on the bottom, so that it extends over the cut side, to show whether the side and the bottom will join nicely together. If not, a bit more touch-up with the sander may be in order. Once the sanding is complete, inspect the packing tape at each of the forms for damage. If the tape has been cut into, slip some new tape pieces under the planks to cover the damaged areas. We definitely do not want to glue the hull to the forms.

We are now ready to install the bottom. First, tape the 2 longest planks (13 and 1/2 feet) together along their length using packing tape, leaving the last foot or so tape-free, so that the planks can be glued to the sides at the stems. Lay these 2 planks, tape side down, along the centerline V-shape on the forms. Screw the planks to the forms, after applying a bead of glue on the side edges that the planks will rest on, and tack the bottom planks to the glued edges of the side planks at the stems using the small nails, or pull them down tightly with packing tape. Apply glue to the next plank edge, and to the side edge, and install it with screws. Apply hot glued stick pieces as necessary to keep the planks in proper alignment, again, remembering to avoid placing hot-glued pieces in the center where the fiberglass tape will be installed. For all of the bottom planks, be sure to glue them to the edges of the side planks, and tack them down using small nails or strap them down with packing tape, as necessary. If using tape, it helps to pull the tape clear down to the shear and wrap it around inside of the hull.

Since the bottom is relatively flat, except for at the stems, I find that the bottom planks tend to mate nicely with each other simply by manipulating them a bit by hand prior to screwing them down. Do not try to trim the excess wood hanging past the sides at this point. Be patient and let the glue dry before trimming the excess bottom wood along the chine. Trimming the sides and installing the bottom takes 3- 4 hours.

Making a Ripple

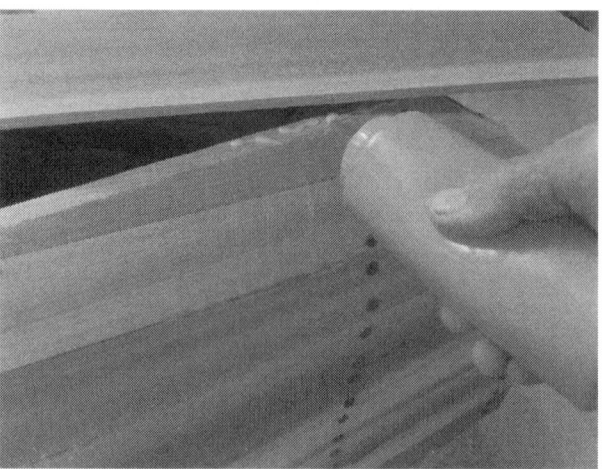

To trim the bottom, place paneling nails just outside of the side/ bottom joint at each of the forms. Using the batten, sweep this arc, tack it down at each end, and scribe it with a pencil. Be sure that this line- at all points- is outside of the side/bottom joint; the excess wood remaining after the saw cut can be removed with the belt sander. Using the circular saw- with the blade set at just over 1/4"- carefully cut along this line, being sure that all of the screws and nails that could be hit by the saw blade have been removed. Using a belt sander with a new 80 grit belt, sand the overhanging wood almost flush, following the contour of the sides. Finish sanding the bottom/side joint using the random orbital sander with a 60 grit disc, being sure to continue the contour of the side to the bottom of the canoe.

Strapping the Hull Together

The hull is now formed with the planks, but it is not worth risking the removal of the screws just yet. To be safe, we will apply straps of fiberglass tape, from shear to shear, between the forms. There will be a total of 10 straps holding the hull together. I use wood glue instead of ep-

oxy resin at this point. The wood glue is non-toxic, less expensive, and the edges of the fiberglass tape are easy to feather by sanding once the glue is dry. When the glue dries, it tends to pull the tape tightly against the wood; almost as if it has been vacuum-formed onto it. First, sand the bed area for the tape using 60 grit discs on the orbital sander, and round the chine as it will eventually be rounded for the remainder of the hull, since there will be no sanding under the tape once it is installed. It is an important step to take the time to round the chine nicely in the area being covered by the tape, since rounding of the chine will continue once the screws are removed, and we want it all to be uniform in appearance. Thicken about 2 ounces of glue with sanding dust and fill any gaps- especially at the stems-that will be covered with the tape, using a plastic spreader. Then spread wood glue onto the tape bed with a brush, apply the tape, brush more glue over the tape to saturate the mesh, and scrape off the excess glue with a plastic spreader. It takes roughly 12 ounces of wood glue to complete this task.

Once the straps are installed, the stems must be glued together so the screws can all be removed (the next day). The stem joint, as it nears the canoe bottom, tends to close-up, and may need some widening by making cuts with the Japanese saw (without cutting into the packing tape), prior to forcing thickened epoxy into the joint. Mix up about 3 ounces of epoxy resin, thicken it with wood flour (harvested from the orbital sander), and pack the stem joint with it.

The resin should cure sufficiently over-night to allow for the removal of all the screws.

Shaping the Hull

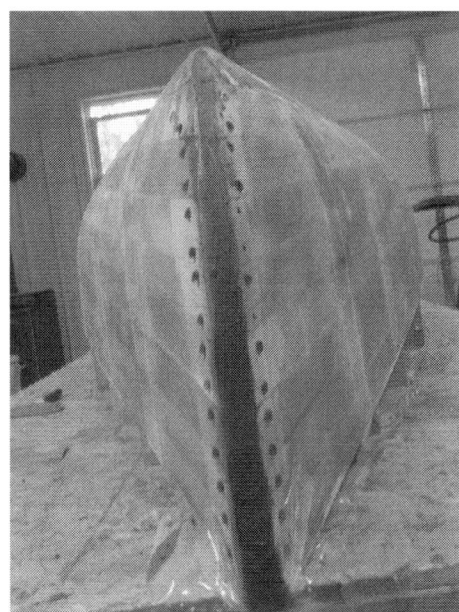

Now that the screws are all out, it is time to make a bit of a mess. Start with the belt sander equipped with a new 80 grit belt, and rough-sand the hull. Concentrate on shaping the chine, but avoid cutting through the fiberglass tape. Then switch to a 60 grit disc on the orbital sander to finish shaping the chine and smooth the hull. The entire hull sanding and shaping process is a matter of preference for the builder. Some may strive for a near- showroom appearance, while most of us will opt for a pretty decent looking hull, with enough imperfections to keep our friends happily pointing them out. It helps to keep in mind, during the entire building process, that this is a wooden craft; it is not a factory-made fiberglass production hull that is popped out of a mold. Wood is a natural product, and most folks understand that a wooden boat should look like it is made of wood.

A good initial hull sanding should take less than an hour. Concentrate on the chine, and round it nicely for a smooth transition from the side to the bottom. Using the Rockwell Vibra-Free sander I am able to sand the entire bottom using just one 60 grit sanding disc, unless there is too much hot glue residue left on the hull, since this residue gums-up the disc fairly quickly. It therefore pays to scrape as much hot glue off as possible with the heat gun and scraper prior to sanding.

Making a Ripple

The 12 ounce fiberglass cloth will even-out most minor imperfections, so no more than an hour of sanding should be required at this point. Between forms #1 and #2 there may be a slight hump (this is also the spot where the gap between the center planks is at its widest). This is more of an illusion than a real hump, but it can be easily taken down some with the sander.

Filling Gaps and Holes

After sanding the hull to reduce flat spots, uneven plank alignments and glue globs, clean the hull using the leaf blower (if ventilation is adequate) followed by a wipe-down with a microfiber

cloth, then mix up 6 ounces of epoxy resin and thicken it with blended filler. Blended filler is a dry mixture of micro-balloons and colloidal silica. Micro-balloons are tiny phenolic spheres that thicken the resin. Even when thickened, however, the resin will sag as gravity pulls it glacially to earth. This is where the colloidal silica comes in; it helps to defy gravity and reduce the sags and runs in the uncured resin. I find that about 3/4 cup of blended filler to 6 ounces of resin is about right.

Apply the thickened resin using a modified 12" taping knife, being certain that the screw-holes are all being filled. The taping knife is modified by removing the metal strap from the top of the blade, which is there to stiffen it. We want our blade to bend and conform to the rounded shape of the hull. To remove the strap, cut through it on each side, as close to the handle as possible, using a cut-off wheel on a Dremel tool, a metal cutting blade on an angle grinder, or a hacksaw. Once cut through, tap-off the strap.

Pour the entire contents from the container along one side of the bottom. Grab a bit of thickened resin with the taping knife and apply good pressure to pull it up from the shear to the canoe bottom, covering the side in this manner. Then spread the thickened resin along the bottom. If there is excess resin, transfer it over to the other side. It will likely require another 6 ounces of thickened resin to complete the other side of the hull. Use a flexible spreader to distribute the resin along the chine.

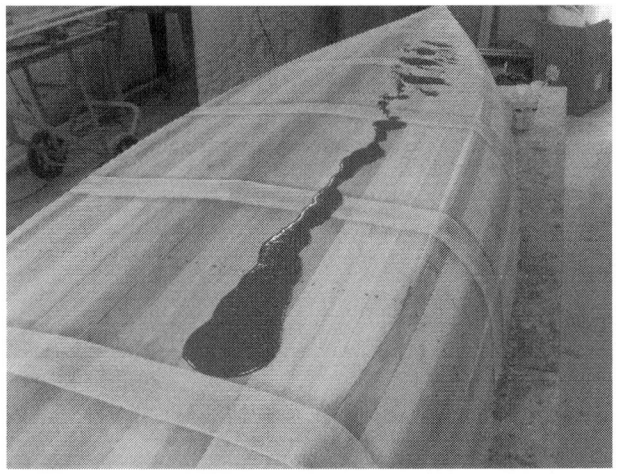

Try to avoid leaving resin to drip and harden on the underside of the shear. Some of this is unavoidable, but we need to distinguish the true shear from accumulated resin when it comes time to attach the gunwales.

There will likely be some thickened resin remaining once the hull has been coated. Add some more blended filler to further thicken the resin, and, using a flexible spreader, pull this mixture up along the stems to give them a nicely rounded shape.

Installing the Fiberglass Cloth

Once the thickened resin has cured, sand the bottom again in preparation for the fiberglass cloth. It is worth waiting for well-cured resin (about 24 hours), which will then sand easily. There is no need to get too carried away with the sanding at this point. The fiberglass cloth will cover minor dips and holes, which will be followed by 2-3 coats of filler. This sanding session takes only about 15 minutes. After sanding, blow off the dust with a leaf blower (if you can open the doors), and then wipe the hull down with a microfiber cloth to get it mostly dust-free.

Roll out the 50" wide biaxial cloth so that it extends to the tips of the stems on each end. If you bought just 5 yards of cloth, then no cutting should be necessary. If you bought enough for other projects (such as another canoe), then cut the cloth after being certain that it will reach to the stem tips on each end. Drape the cloth so that it just reaches the shear on each side. Use a permanent marker to mark the centerline in several spots so that the cloth can be easily centered once it is re-applied. Trim the excess cloth from the stem sections, and then roll the cloth up and set it aside. Mix up 12 ounces of resin to coat the hull, and distribute it evenly with the metal taping knife and brush. I have found that mixing up 6 to 12 ounces of resin at a time is a good amount to work with, and greatly reduces the risk of having the whole container harden up in a matter of minutes. The more resin/hardener molecules that are in contact with each other in a small space, the more heat that will be generated as bonds are formed and energy is released

Making a Ripple

as a by-product of the exothermic reaction; it's a bit like packing too many guys into the fish house, without the smell.

With the entire hull uniformly wetted with resin, roll the cloth out, along the centerline, so that it drapes evenly on each side of the canoe. It will reach about to the shear on each side. Smooth the cloth onto the hull using your gloved hands. Cut the cloth that bulges up at the stems so that it will lay flat. Do not try to get the cloth to wrap around the stems; we will tape them later. Mix 12 ounces of epoxy resin

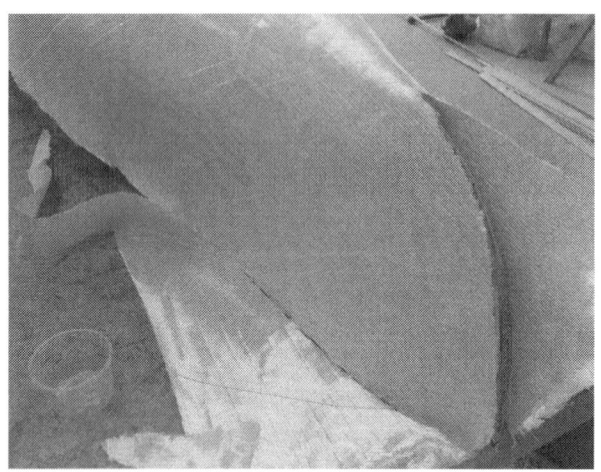

and pour it onto the cloth on the flat part of the bottom; then, using a brush and the metal taping knife, work from the pooled resin to distribute it. Since we will be mixing 12 ounces of resin about 6 times to saturate the fabric, I find that creating a graduated container helps to streamline the process. Pour 8 ounces of water into a container, mark the waterline with a permanent marker, add 4 more ounces of water and mark this line. Then dump out the water and dry the container well. Now we only need to fill to the bottom line with resin, to the top line with hardener, mix well and pour the contents onto the canoe bottom for distribution. Saturate the fabric, but do not over-fill the weave. Mix up more resin to saturate the weave in one section, and move on to the next section. It will take about 72 ounces of resin to saturate the fabric. You will know that the cloth (fabric) has received enough resin when it turns from white to clear. Using the taping knife allows you to apply plenty of resin quickly and efficiently, whereas applying resin with

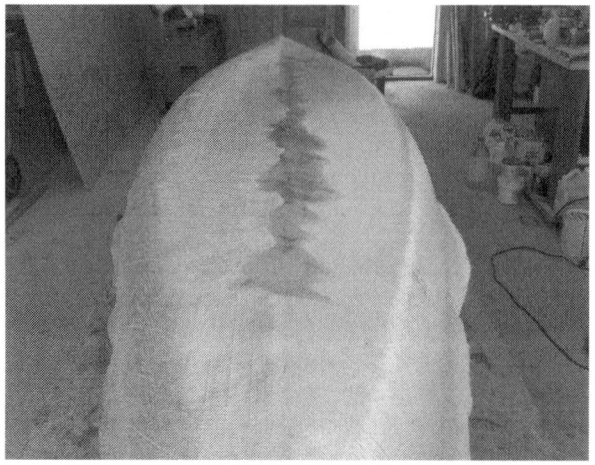

only a brush uses far too much resin and takes far too long to apply. Watch for air pockets under the fabric; especially at the chine and along the keel. The brush is used primarily to deal with these trapped air bubbles. Dab at the air pockets with the brush and work them out from under the fabric. Filling the weave with resin is the step that uses the bulk of the epoxy resin; which is understandable, since the 12 ounce cloth, once filled with more than a half gallon of cured resin, becomes the impressively strong, lightweight and durable outer hull of the canoe. Apply good pressure to the taping knife to force excess resin out of the fabric, since a fairly lean ratio of resin to fiberglass makes for a stronger hull. It is also much easier to sand the surface, once it cures, if there is no cured resin pooled above the surface of the fabric.

Once the resin has cured -usually over-night- sand the entire surface with a 60 grit sanding disc on the orbital sander. This is only a light sanding intended to knock-down glass fibers and any high spots, in preparation for filling the weave with thickened resin. The color of the fabric will change from clear to powdery-white once the surface has been lightly sanded. Remember not to sand too heavily, especially along the chine or the keel; we do not want to sand through the fabric, and compromise its strength, where it is needed the most. This sanding session takes only a few minutes. A micro-fiber cloth is good at picking up dust and can be used to wipe the hull surface clean and dust-free.

Once the stems are rounded and sanded, they will need to be taped so that we can sleep at night without fear of them spontaneously springing open. Cut a piece of fiberglass tape to cover the entire length of each stem, mix about 2 ounces of resin, brush it on the stem, apply the tape with gloved hands, and apply enough resin, using a brush, to saturate the weave of the tape.

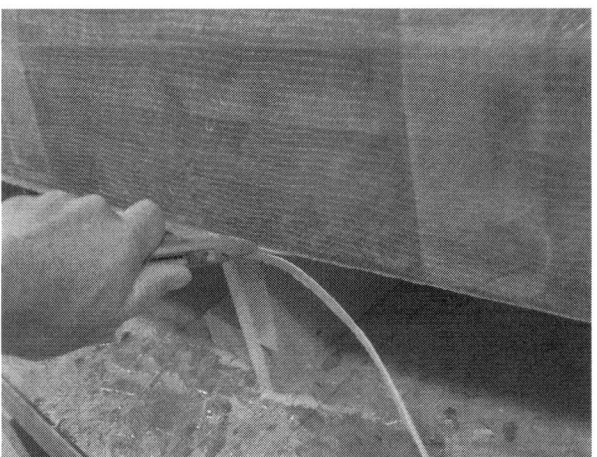

Once the taped stems have cured they are sanded and shaped using the fairing compound. The stem will eventually also be taped on the inside; meaning the canoe can likely be used as an ice breaker.

Fairing the Hull

Mix up 6 ounces of resin, and add enough blended filler to create a spreadable mixture; about ¾ of a cup of blended filler mixed into 6 ounces of resin is about right. This coat is intended to fill-in most of the weave of the cloth without causing too much sagging and sanding. The blended filler is used as an economical way to fill the weave of the fabric, and since it is stronger than the more expensive fairing compound, which we will save for the final fairing of the hull. Apply the thickened resin by pouring the entire contents along one side of the canoe bottom. As with the application of thickened resin prior to installing the cloth, take a dab of resin from the puddle and pull it up from the shear. Mix another 6 ounces of resin and repeat the spreading process on the other side of the canoe. Twelve ounces should be about the right amount of thickened resin to coat the entire hull. While applying the resin bend the knife to conform to the curve of the side. Scrape excess resin from the knife back into the container following each pass. Use a flexible spreader to distribute resin along the chine. There should be a small amount of resin remaining after the hull is coated, which can be further thickened with blended filler to apply to the stems. Place a glob of thickened resin on a flexible spreader, and pull the material up along the entire stem, creating a nicely rounded shape that will fill the weave of the fiberglass tape.

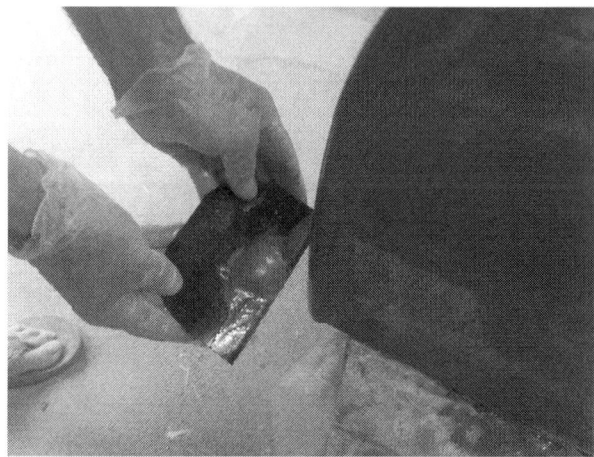

It helps at this point to remember that it is much simpler, and more economical, to apply a couple of thin coats-with light sanding between them- than it is to apply a heavy coat, and spend far too much time sanding it off again. Once a layer has cured, sand the hull, being careful not to cut into the weave, especially at the chine and stems. If a considerable amount of the weave is still apparent, a second coat of thickened epoxy will likely be in order. The weave of the fiberglass cloth runs predominately parallel to the floor, so pulling the filler up, from the shear to the keel, leaves a bit of a washboard look as the taping knife is pulled perpendicular to the weave of the fabric. The second coat of filler should be pulled horizontally, from stem to stem, to fill the washboard depressions. This coat of thickened epoxy should take about 9 ounces of resin and about a cup of blended filler. Spread about 1/2 of the contents on each side of the canoe bottom, and, as before, dab some with the knife, and pull it up from the shear over the chine.

Once the entire canoe has been coated in this manner, then start at one stem and pull the knife horizontally along the shear, while forcefully bending the knife to conform to the hull. Scrape excess resin from the knife into the container, and make another horizontal pull mid-way along the canoe side. Finish the side with a third horizontal pull along the chine. Then pull the knife along the canoe bottom, from stem to stem, scraping excess resin back into the container. Use the flexible spreader (the one made from vinyl baseboard about 4" wide works well here) to smooth-out the resin along the chine, from stem to stem. Use some excess resin on the flexible spreader to dress-up the stems.

Once the resin has cured, a light sanding with a 120 grit disc is in order prior to the final fairing of the hull. The hull could be finished using a third coat of thickened resin with good results, but the fairing compound is worth the added cost, in my opinion, to quickly give the hull a finish that has folks wondering if it really is a wooden canoe. Fairing compound spreads easily, and a little bit goes a long way, as long as there is not too much weave yet to fill. It is also a breeze to sand, and cures quickly. It takes a bit of practice to become adept at pulling a smooth, even, thin layer of fairing compound length-wise from stem to stem without leaving voids that are deficient in compound, however. It is important that the hull is free of sanding dust prior to applying the fairing compound, since it picks up the dust and becomes too stiff if it is worked too much. The fairing compound is applied horizontally just as the thickened epoxy was applied, with the flexible spreader used along the chine and stems. Once cured, a light sanding with a 120 grit disc on the orbital sander is in order. Applying firm pressure to the taping knife blade while pulling it from stem to stem fills areas deficient in resin without leaving too much cured fairing compound that needs to be sanded off. Sanding is not the most enjoyable part of the project, so minimizing it is prudent. The fairing compound, once sanded, turns powdery white, and depressions that were passed-over by the sander will remain a darker color, and therefore detectable. Some persistent sanding over these areas may fair the surface; but if it does not, this area deficient in compound should be touched-up with a bit more fairing compound, unless their presence does not concern you.

Re-coating the entire hull with a second coat of fairing compound is hopefully not necessary,

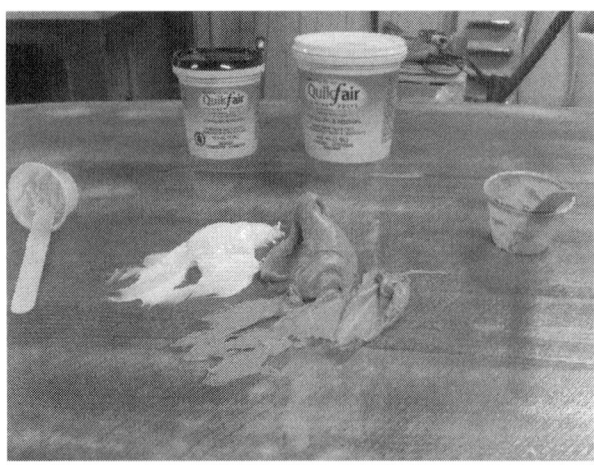

since that gets to be a lot of mostly unnecessary sanding. Touching- up the depressions and perhaps dressing-up the stems a bit more may be in order, however. Mixing up about 2 ounces of fairing compound should be enough to hit those spots, which will require additional sanding with the orbital sander, followed by a quick sanding session by hand. Sanding by hand enables you to feel the surface with the palm of your hand and detect any remaining high or low spots that may require more attention.

Once the hull is as fair as your pride will allow, a final coat of epoxy resin is required over the sanded fairing compound to saturate and harden it prior to a final very light sanding, primer and paint. The best method I have found to apply the epoxy resin is to use the combination of the brush, taping knife and a 4" foam roller. Mix up 6 ounces of resin, pour it out onto the canoe bottom, and brush a strip along about a 4' section of the shear on one side of the hull. Using the taping knife, pull the resin up and over the chine, and maybe even over the keel. Repeat until the entire side has been coated with resin, and then coat the other side in the same manner. The entire hull can be covered quickly with less than 6 ounces of resin. As the resin is pulled up and over the chine to the keel, and there is resin remaining on the knife edge, scrape the excess resin back into the container. Once the entire hull has been evenly coated using the taping knife, brush some resin onto the foam roller so that you are not starting the rolling process out dry, and distribute the resin on the hull using the roller. The roller evens-out the resin that was spread with the taping knife, removes the ridges inevitably left when a fairly flat blade is pulled along a curved hull, and results in a smooth, even coat of resin that minimizes the dreaded runs and sags that appear out of nowhere whenever we are using epoxy resin. There will likely be a couple of ounces of extra resin in the container once the hull is coated. Resist the temptation to use this remaining resin on the hull. It will only cause problems. As annoying as it is to waste resin, just let it cure in the container, unless you are a better planner than I am, and have another project handy that needs a few ounces of epoxy.

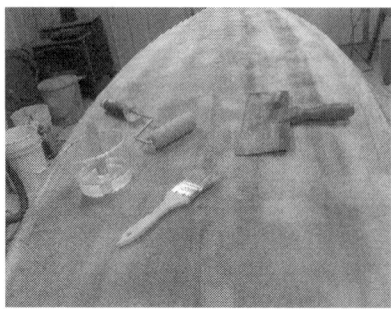

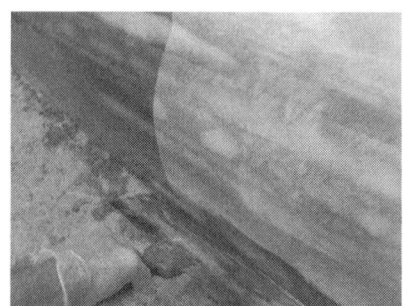

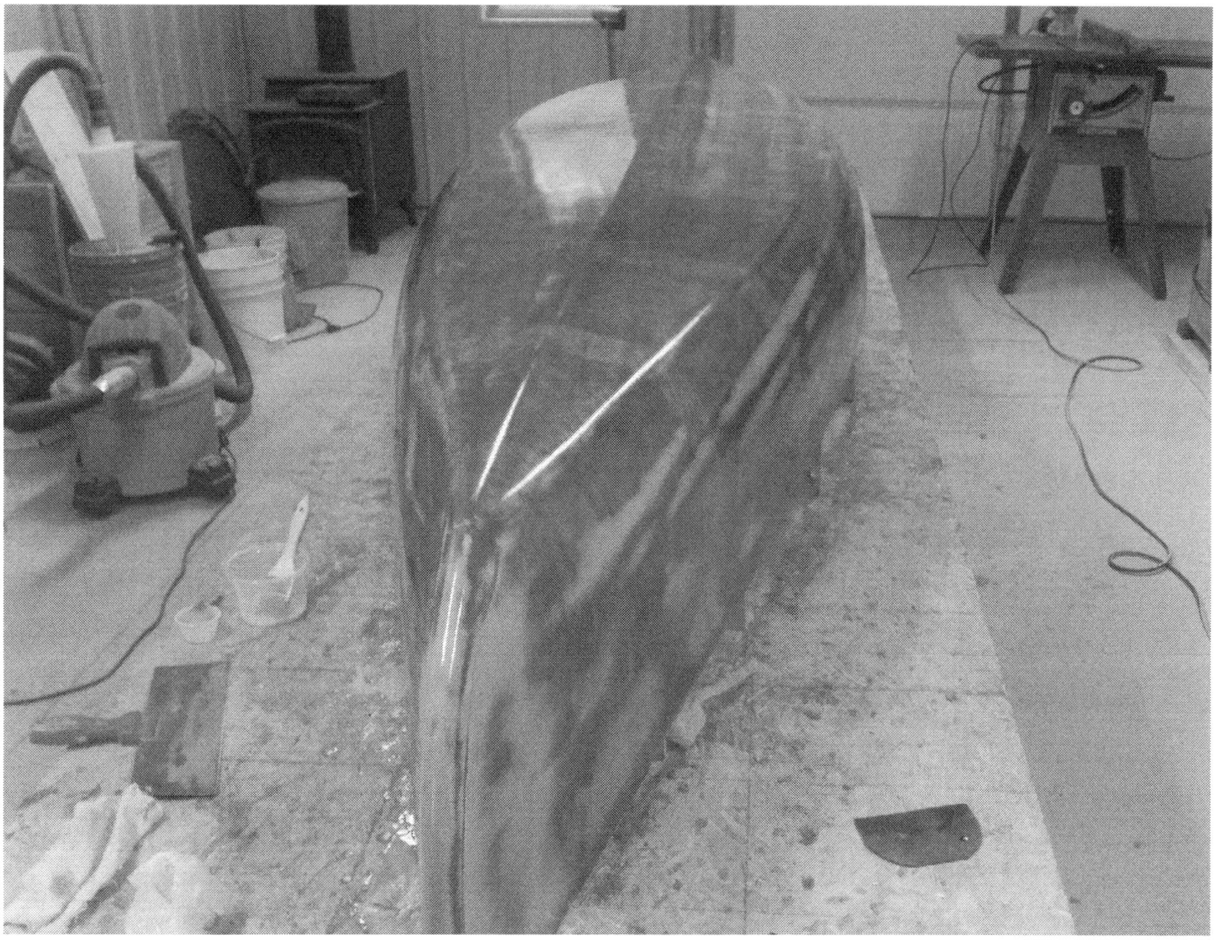

Attaching the Gunwales

When the hull is good enough, it is time to install the gunwales. I like to do this while the hull is still nestled on its forms, since the forms provide good support to bend the wood around without fear of misshaping the hull. I like the look of a 1"deep x ½" thick gunwale, but for the pine canoe I used 1/2"x3/4" gunwales with nice results. I did this because I made the gunwales out of pine, and that was all that I had left from the 2x4s that I had ripped for the planks. If you choose a hardwood, such as ash, for the gunwales, there may be some scarf joints to make, since 16' long knot-free hardwood boards may be difficult (and expensive) to come by.

Making a Ripple

Otherwise, pine gunwales look nice; or they can also be ripped from cedar, which will be soft, and subject to dings, but I do not think that is much of an issue, since this is hopefully not a canoe to be rattling around in the bed of a pick-up. Both the gunwale and the hull along the shear are brushed with epoxy resin (about an ounce and a half should do it). The gunwale is then clamped amidships (in the middle) with a spring clamp, then clamped at

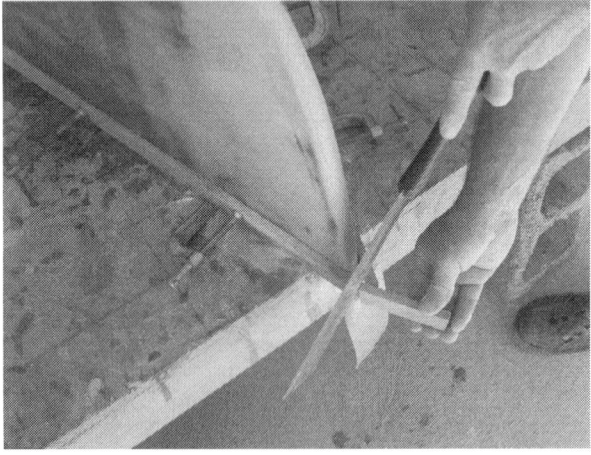

one end as close to the stem as possible with a spring clamp. Work from this end, clamping as you go with the spring clamps, to install the gunwale flush with the shear. This gets a bit difficult if too much resin had been deposited along the shear. It is best to minimize the drips and runs in the first place, but if hardened epoxy obscures the true shear, at least sand a few areas to the bare wood every 2 feet or so to help guide you in the proper installation of the gunwale along the shear. I use spring clamps, initially, to hold the gunwale where it needs to be, then go back and install C-clamps as close to the stem as possible, and wherever it appears that the gunwale needs some help lying snugly against the side of the canoe. I use 15 spring clamps (because I only have 30 of them), and 6 C-clamps (because I only have a dozen of them) per side. Cut the excess wood from the stem, leaving about 1" of wood extending past it. We need to leave a bit of wood overhanging the stems so we can put a wood screw through it to serve as a clamp to draw the gunwales together at the stems. Leave enough extra wood to do this, but do not leave so much that it interferes with the installation of the gunwale on the other side of the hull. Once the gunwales on both sides are clamped in place, drill a pilot hole through the excess wood, and install a wood screw to snug-up the gunwales nicely against the hull; but do not over-tighten them or the gunwales will bulge out a foot or so back from the stems.

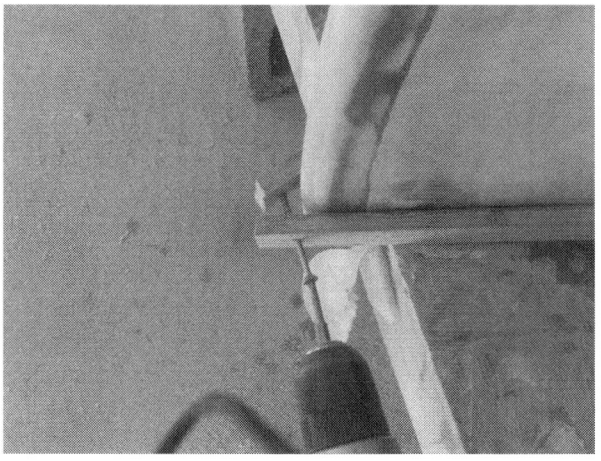
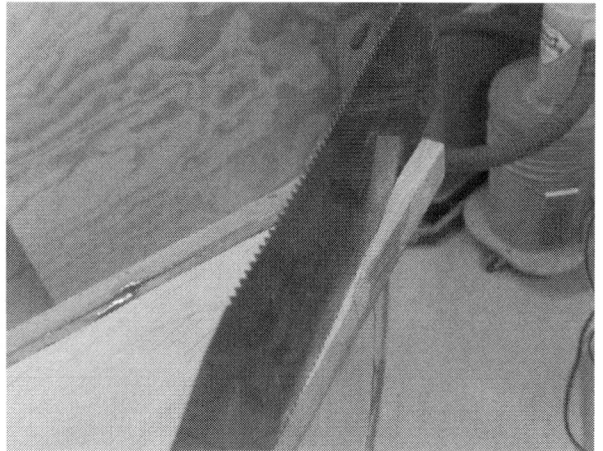

Once the resin has cured, the clamps and screws are removed and the excess wood is lopped off, angling back from the stem, using the Japanese saw.

The Long-Awaited Flipping of the Canoe

With the gunwales installed, the flipping of the hull is the big next step. This can be performed most easily, once again, with an assistant. But, if you are like me, this is a sacred moment best performed alone with your creation. Anyway, the hull should pop off the form fairly easily, and the canoe will be fairly light (although a bit flimsy) at this point. A pair of saw horses, with boards laid along their outside edges, makes a good work surface for the following tasks, which are really outdoor activities, if at all possible. Otherwise, the forms can be modified to serve as a cradle for the up-right canoe. Simply clamp boards, about 4' in length, to the tops of the #5 forms; then lay boards across the clamped boards on each side. The canoe sits a bit too high for effective interior sanding, however.

The inside is going to require sanding, and, depending on how careful you were at aligning and gluing the planks, this can be a tedious task. Regardless, it will be a messy task, and the shape of the hull makes looking down while sanding a great way to fill one's eyes with sanding dust. Start with a 60 grit sanding disc, and the shaping goes well without much gouging. Sanding the inside of the canoe is the least pleasant part of the whole project, in my opinion, so get it over with as efficiently as possible by using care when building the hull, by sanding with

good quality discs, and by replacing them as they lose their effectiveness. The canoe floor, being fairly flat, is easily sanded. The sides are another matter; being curved, the sander spends a lot of its time tilted at an angle, to conform to the curved surface. Use care when sanding with a 60 grit disc, since cedar is soft and easily gouged if one lingers too long on one spot with the sander tilted at an angle. It may take a couple of hours to complete the task, but then the worst part of the whole project will be over. Once the inside surface is sanded with the coarse disc, go over it with a 120 grit disc to smooth it out. The sander will not fit into the stems, meaning the last foot or so of the sides must be sanded by hand. This should be enough hand sanding for you to develop a great appreciation for a 5" random orbital sander. The good news is that the stem sections will be under the stem decks, and not be too visible; only to the hyper-observant eyes of that good friend of yours who will joyfully point out the globs of unsanded wood glue at the stems. Be sure to leave enough to keep him (or her, if you are married) happy.

Covering the Canoe Floor, Chine and Stems

The 12 ounce cloth covering the outside of the canoe results in an impressively strong fiberglass hull that eliminates (I believe) the need for covering the entire inside of the canoe with fiberglass; except for on the floor. I would not be comfortable leaving the floor unsheathed with fiberglass; for reasons of both strength and durability. But, to keep the weight, and cost, down, I use only 4 ounce cloth on the floor.

Before doing any work on the inside of the canoe, however, the true hull shape must be restored. Once freed from the forms, the hull pulls together a bit. Cut a 36" piece of wood to act as a temporary thwart to restore the true beam, or install the wood blank that will become the thwart. Doing this will change the shape of the bottom slightly to its true shape. The best method I have found to install the cloth is to first lay it out on the clean, dry canoe floor, rough-trim the excess from the stems, and then

 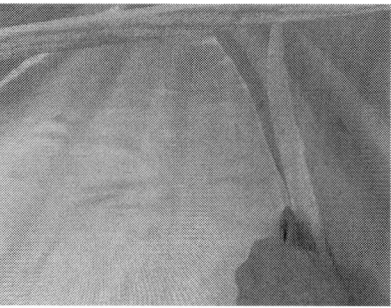 

cut-out the football shape along the chine using a razor knife. Now carefully roll back half of the fabric onto itself, spread 6 ounces of resin onto the bare bottom with a taping knife and brush, and gently roll the fabric back down, working out air pockets and creases as you work toward the stem using your gloved hands, and a plastic spreader, if necessary. Working with thin 4 ounce cloth can be frustrating, so work slowly and carefully. Repeat the process for the other side of the bottom, using another 6 ounces of resin. Mix 3 more ounces of resin to saturate the weave of the fabric. Fifteen ounces of resin should be enough to install the cloth.

Once the resin on the canoe floor is cured, a fillet of epoxy resin thickened with wood-flour is then applied to the chine joint. Mix up 6 ounces of resin and add enough sanding dust to give it a thick, but spreadable, consistency. Use a rounded flexible spreader, cut from a plastic container, such as a milk jug, and pull small amounts of the material along with it. There should be enough mixture remaining to spread a fillet in the stems. A craft stick works well to apply the thickened resin in the stems. Once the radius is formed with the thickened resin, a coat of un-thickened resin (6 ounces) is lightly applied over it using a brush. Three inch wide fiberglass tape is then laid over the fillet, and saturated with more resin; being careful to avoid pressing down too hard with the brush and misshaping the fillet. It is best to lay the tape down dry, cut it to length and roll it back up, so it can be rolled out along the chine once it is wetted with resin. Partially unroll the tape along the dry bottom before laying it down, and see if it has a tendency to curve on way or the other once it is unrolled. If so, use this to your advantage by having the natural curve of the tape coincide with the curve of the chine. Another 6 ounces of resin will be needed to finish saturating the tape along the chine and stems (the stem tape pieces are best pre-cut, too).

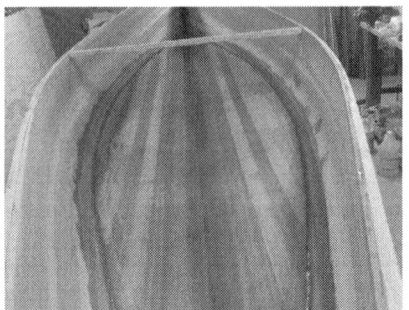

Once saturated, the taped chine joint can be finished by pulling a flat plastic spreader lightly downward across the tape and onto the canoe bottom. This tends to eliminate any air pockets, reduces runs, and helps to re-shape the fillet. Once the resin is cured, the edges of the tape can be feathered using the orbital sander.

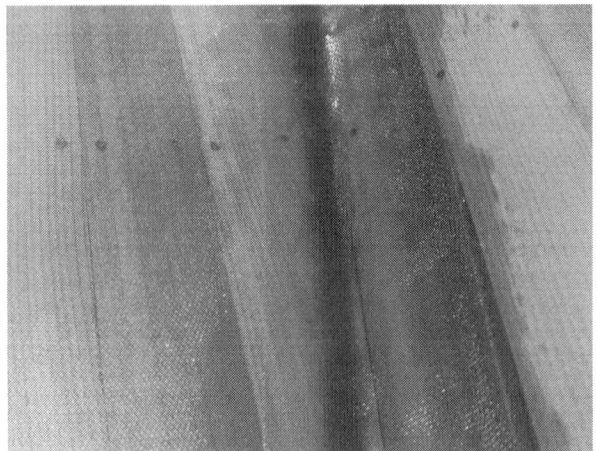

Installing Ribs

A possibly unnecessary task that I am not willing to eliminate is to install ribs over the screw holes on the floor at the center and the #5 and #4 form locations, for a total of 5 ribs. I do this thinking it helps as a stiffener to keep the bottom from undulating like a waterbed while in the water, but perhaps I am being a bit over-cautious. Regardless, they are easy to install, they cover the screw holes, they look kind of nice, and they provide some traction on the otherwise smooth canoe floor; so I am for keeping them in the plans. The ribs are simply remnant pieces of plank that have been cut to fit inside of the taped chine, and are rounded on the ends to resemble giant

tongue depressors. A cut is made, using the Japanese saw, most of the way, but not all the way, through the center so that the rib hinges and conforms to the V-shape in the canoe bottom. Epoxy resin is then brushed onto the canoe bottom where the rib will go, and to the rib. A piece of scrap wood (1"x1" works well) is then spring clamped to the gunwales over the rib being glued to the floor. Two (or more if necessary) short pieces of scrap plank are then pushed onto the rib to hold it down, and are spring-clamped to the bar across the canoe. This requires a bit of patience, since pushing down too hard on one temporary brace tends to loosen another as the canoe bottom and the clamping rod flex. The soft wood is not covered with fiberglass cloth, so it becomes prone to dings from any rough treatment, but I like to simply avoid rough treatment of the canoe in the first place. This is a durable canoe, but it is not one that should be battered around like the dented aluminum ones that rock around in the beds of the pick-up trucks of our local leech harvesters.

Interior Gunwales, Stem Decks and Thwart

We now have a strong canoe but we need to stiffen it a bit more, and, unfortunately, make it heavier. To do this we must install the inside portion of the gunwale (the inwale), and the stem decks (also called breasthooks- which sounds painful). The inwale is clamped to the inside just as the gunwale was attached, but it will end where

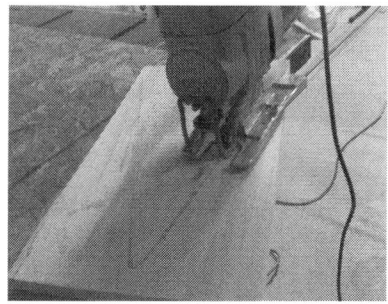

it joins the stem decks. To make the stem decks I plane some 6" wide hardwood down to ½", and, using a biscuit joiner, glue the planks together (or join first, then plane down). Or, if 8" wide board is available, it eliminates the need for joinery. Good quality 1/2" plywood would be good material for stem decks, if one is not opposed to looking at the plies on the exposed edge. Plywood would be strong, and also eliminate the need to join 2 pieces of wood.

To fashion stem decks, lay the ½" boards over the stems and trace the triangular shape from underneath. I do not think that a large stem deck is necessary, and measure back about 12" along the gunwales from the tip of the stem to mark the back of the stem deck. Cut the shape out using a saber saw, being careful to cut outside of the line. The piece will require sanding to get it to fit snugly into the stem, and I find a stationary disc/belt sander to be the best tool for this task. If you do not own such a machine, it can certainly be done using the orbital sander, or, if done carefully, the belt sander. Then notch out a bit (1/2"x1/2") for the inwale, which will extend slightly inside the stem deck. Once the deck fits nicely, use four #6 brass or stainless steel screws that are 1 and 1/2" in length, countersunk into the gunwale, to hold the deck in place. *Later, when the canoe is flipped over, we will apply a fillet of epoxy, thickened with wood flour, and fiberglass tape to secure and strengthen the deck on its underside. The top side of the deck will, unless you are much more meticulous than I am, require some filler around the edges. When resin is mixed for the inwale, save back a small amount and thicken it with sanding dust to fill the gaps around the stem decks. Once the decks are installed, a hole is drilled, centered on the deck, back 4" or so from the stem, for attaching lines and the trailer hitch tongue; should a trailer be desired. Drilling holes in your work may seem extreme, but remember, it is a canoe meant to be used, not a showpiece. A neat 3/8" hole in each end allows for a line to be attached to the bow, and the trailer tongue to be attached to the stern end. The position of the seats allows the hitch to have some tongue weight for towing behind a bicycle when pulled from the stern.

The inwale can now be installed, after first cutting it to fit into the notches on the stem decks. They can most easily be installed before mounting the stem decks. With the stem decks temporarily held in place, mark the inside of the notch on the gunwale, and remove the stem decks. Clamp the inwale temporarily in position and mark where it needs to be cut. This only works if the inwale is clamped tightly against the side to get an accurate measurement (I know this from experience). The inwale is then installed just as the gunwale was installed; but try to avoid using too much resin, since it will then run and harden inside the canoe.

The thwart can be a simple, straight, piece of wood, but I like a bit of curve to it, so I cut out a bit on each side to give it a more traditional look; I then router the edges to round them off nicely. It only takes about 10 minutes to turn a flat board into a nicely shaped thwart. To fashion a thwart I start with a 36"x3" piece of 3/4" thick wood, draw a pencil line 4" in from the ends on each side, and another line 14" in from the ends on each side. Midway between these marks (9" in from the ends) measure in about 3/8" from the edge, tack a small brad in place, and sweep an arc with a mini batten. Cut the shallow radius out on a band saw. I found one thwart, installed amidships, to be the best arrangement for this canoe. For longer portages, you can also fashion a yoke into the thwart. Ash is my preferred wood for the stem decks, thwart and seat frames. I like it because it is a strong, straight-grained, and beautiful wood. Unfortunately, the Emerald Ash Borer is doing its best to take this wonderful tree from us. As of this writing it is yet confined to the southern portion of Minnesota; perhaps that is one reason to not grumble so much about our recent severe winters. Any wood strong enough to perform as a thwart, stem deck, or seat frame can be used in their construction. I used cottonwood for the thwart, stem plates and seat frames on the pine canoe, with surprisingly nice results, since my cousin had milled some and given it to me awhile back.

Being resourceful (cheap) I decided to try it, rather than purchase ash or other hardwood. I imagine that poplar or basswood would also work well; especially basswood, being fine grained with few knots. Remember that the length of the thwart is the true beam (36"). The thwart can be installed below the inwale, or a bit can be notched out of the thwart for the inwale.

Finishing the Interior

A few more light sanding sessions are now in order to sand the gunwales, stem decks, and any spots that are not to your satisfaction (within reason) in the interior. The entire interior, along with the gunwales, stem decks and thwart, are then covered with about 12 ounces of resin. Pour the entire contents down the center of the floor and use the brush, taping knife and foam roller method to quickly and evenly distribute the resin. Once the resin has cured, a light sanding is in order with fine sandpaper, and then covered with a coat or 2 of spar varnish. If you feel that the wood needs a bit more protection, a second coat of resin may be applied prior to applying the spar varnish. The spar varnish is used to protect the resin from the effects of the sun; it is kind of like applying sunscreen to the canoe. Most epoxy has no UV protection, and will yellow and degrade over time when exposed to sunlight. The spar varnish has UV protection that protects the epoxy finish. The varnish will also degrade over time in direct sunlight, but it should not be a concern for many years, or decades. There are now water-based spar varnishes available which I prefer to the oil based varnish, which tends to take a long time to dry, and requires the use of solvents to clean the brushes. Alternately, you are free to paint the interior of the canoe, but then the wood grain is hidden away, and we really should show it off a bit. You are not leaving your canoe sitting outside, right? There is no excuse to store a small, relatively light craft such as this one outdoors. I have noticed that, even when stored upside down outside, the morning dew forms on the inside of the canoe. Hang it from the rafters, if there is no room to hang it on the wall of a garage or pole barn, but please do not store it, or any boat for that matter, outdoors. Remember, using a vessel is not what wrecks it; sitting outside is what does it in, since nature is relentless in reclaiming and recycling its materials.

Tandem or Single boat.. Double or Single paddle?

Ripple was, at its inception, a solo canoe meant to be paddled with a double- blade paddle while seated on the floor. The canoe, however, proved to be one that could accommodate 2 paddlers. It also proved to be a bit difficult to paddle while seated on the floor, since the gunwales are a bit high for kayak-type paddling without banging the paddle shaft on the gunwales. After performing exhaustive sea-trails (OK, a few trips out on the lake), it was therefore determined that the best configuration for this canoe was a center thwart/yoke with a bow and a stern seat; this arrangement allows one to comfortably paddle solo by sitting backwards in the bow seat.

Seats can be purchased on-line for about $40 apiece (plus shipping). But that is $40 that I feel is needlessly spent, if one is willing and able to make a few simple biscuit or dowel joints in a simple hardwood frame.

While cane seats look nice, a seat made of woven 1" nylon webbing is also attractive, perhaps more practical, less expensive, and easy to install. The bow seat, using 2" wide ash boards that are 3/4" thick, is made from one 32" piece, one of 28", and two that are 8" in length. The outside distance between the 8"cross pieces is 20". The stern seat needs a piece 26", 22" and the two 8" pieces. The distance to the outside of the 8" cross pieces is 18 inches. Once the 2 rung ladder style frame has been joined together as shown in the photos, it is a nice touch to run the router around all of the edges prior to coating them with epoxy, then varnishing and installing the webbing.

Making a Ripple

The webbing is attached on the underside of the frame using stainless steel staples. First determine the spacing (I use about ¼" between each strap), and then start in the center by stapling one end to the inside edge and to the bottom of the frame, pull it tightly to the other side of the frame, and staple to secure. Then cut the webbing using a wood-burning iron with a wide tip, leaving about ¾" so there is enough to put a staple into the inside edge of the frame. Once the process is completed going one direction, repeat the process; this time alternately weaving the webbing through the straps that are already installed.

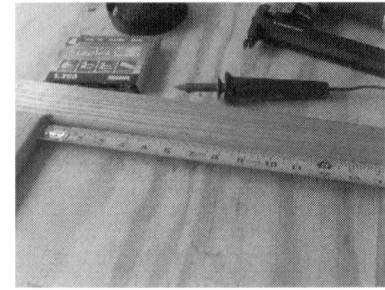

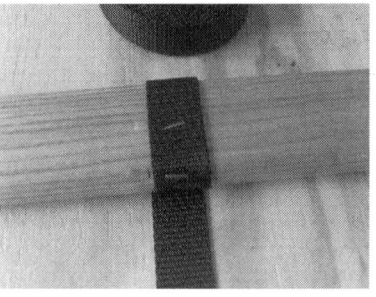

I like the rear of the **stern seat** to be about 3' from the tip of the stem; measured along the gunwale on each side. The rear of the bow seat frame is set at lines drawn 62" back from the tip of the bow stem, along each gunwale. Place the rear frame of each seat on top on the gunwale at these marks, being certain that the seat is centered. Using a straight edge, draw the line at each of the 4 places where the excess frame material will be removed.

44   Making a Ripple

This line will follow the joint between the plank and the inside of the inwale. Once certain that this is where you want to cut, lop off the excess wood with the Japanese saw.

Once the seat frames are cut to size, set the seat just under the inwale, with the rear of the frame even with the marks on the gunwale. Using a marking pen, put a dot, centered on each frame, on the gunwale at the joint between the plank and the inwale. This will be where the 3/16" hole will be drilled for the bolts. Remember to angle the hole slightly inward so that the drill bit emerges on the underside just inside of the planking. For the stern seat cut 2 pieces of 7/32" brass tubing 2" in length, and 2 pieces 1" in length. I find a cutting wheel on a Dremel tool handy for cutting the tubing, although a hack saw works fine. Holding the seat in position, put the drill bit through one of the rear holes, slide a 2" piece of tubing over the bit, and hold the seat frame up against the tubing. Then, using the tubing as a guide, drill into the seat frame. The bit may not be long enough to drill all of the way through the frame, but it will go in far enough for you to finish the hole after repeating the process on the other side. With both rear

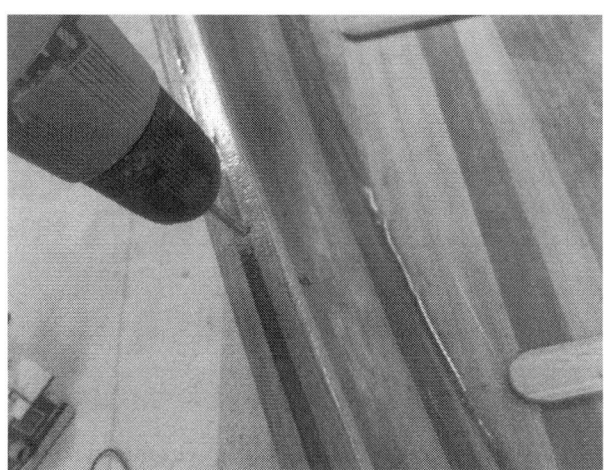

holes drilled, countersink the hole on the top of the gunwale, slide the 4" machine screws through the hole, through the 2" tubing, through the hole in the seat frame, and secure by hand with a washer and lock nut. With the seat somewhat secured, use the 1" brass tubing as guides to drill through the front frame, countersink the hole, and secure with the 3" machine screws. All 4 nuts can now be tightened.

The bow seat is installed using the same method, except that the 4" machine screws, which will be in the front, are covered with only 1 and 1/2" brass tubing. The rear 3" screws are covered with 1" tubing. There will be excess screw extending past the nuts; especially under the bow seat. If this is a concern they can be cut off, but file the cut ends to eliminate sharp edges.

Painting the Hull

Before we paint the hull, a word about why I opted for a design that does not attempt to produce a bright finish that shows-off the wood on the outside (like the cedar strippers do) is in order. First, it is just that; showing off. An exterior resembling a stand-up bass is pretty to look at, but it comes at a great expense in time to attain such a finish. A person can build a new home in the time it takes some builders to meticulously complete a strip canoe. Second, such an exterior, covered only with 6 ounce cloth, is not as durable as one that is protected by 12 ounce fabric impregnated with over 1/2 gallon of epoxy resin. The exterior is where the abuse is taken. It is the part that sits in the water, and encounters all of the objects that are *not* water. It is like the exterior of a car or a house, protecting the interior, where we live. We mostly look at what's on the inside. A bright exterior is not even seen as we paddle our canoe, but the interior is seen, and admired, with every stroke. The $2500 Kevlar canoe may be light and durable, but it is not much to look at as one passes the day inside of it. There is just something pleasing about the look of natural cedar planks accented with hardwood; something that makes us feel like it belongs on a secluded lake or stream.

Now it is time to paint the outside of the canoe. Let me begin this segment by confessing that I am a lousy painter; especially when it comes to using a roller. Having read how a near-perfect finish can be attained by applying oil-based paints using a fine foam roller, I made such an attempt on one of my canoes. This was not my first time painting with a foam roller, since I had previously used this technique to paint the hull of an 18' boat, as well as the 2 ultra-light canoes I had discussed earlier, and I did not recall having much difficulty with the process, using a Top Side marine paint. For some reason-perhaps the paint was old- I ended up with an orange peel texture on my most recent canoe. This was especially frustrating since I

had started with an epoxy coated hull that was admirably smooth and glossy. I knew I was in trouble when I applied the Top Side primer (which is not recommended for use below the waterline-hence the name); transforming the smooth epoxy finish into white stucco. Even worse, the primer-even when completely dry- could not be sanded off using the orbital sander, since the discs clogged with globs of adhered primer after 5 seconds of sanding. I had to sand the entire hull- first with medium grit then with fine grit sandpaper- by hand. Fortunately the primer sands fairly easily by hand, and I finally got the hull back to a smooth condition. The first coat of paint however, applied with a foam roller designed for an ultra-smooth finish, gave me the orange peel look, which subsequent coats (with sanding in between them) did not eliminate.

The point I am trying to make is that, in keeping with the theme of this book (and perhaps my life), achieving a decent appearance should be good enough. Therefore, I suggest leaving the fine-furniture finish to the experts, and go buy a few cans of spray paint for the hull. I have had good luck with the Painter's Touch spray paint in a can, made by Rustoleum. It is inexpensive, quick-drying, and it dries (eventually) to a hard, durable finish. It is also available in some fun colors. The primer goes on first, and does a good job of filling and evening-out small blemishes. If the hull gets some dings, it is easy to fill, sand, prime and re-paint the ding. I did have a bad experience using a red color on one of my canoes, when I attempted to spray it outside on a windy day. The finish was dull in some parts, glossy in others, and even developed cracks in it in places. I was unhappy with the results at the time, but now that the canoe has been used a few times and has received a few well-deserved scratches and a bit of mud on the sides, it just looks like a pretty nice canoe. So the recommendation is for calm winds, or spraying the hull in the workshop-with the doors and windows open.

As with any paint, except for those marine coatings specially formulated for life below the waterline, this paint is not intended to be submerged in water for extended periods.

A canoe is not a vessel that sits moored at a dock overnight, however, so the hull is seldom, if ever, in the water for more than 12 hours. This is not enough time to soften and compromise the painted finish, in my experience. We had kept our boat, painted with Top Side paint, in the water for days at a time with no softening of the finish.

I like to save the hull painting for last, since it feels like the crowning touch to a rewarding project, and the canoe can then sit upside down for a few days to harden without the need to flip it to work more on the interior. Move it out on sunny days to really cook the finish. If you can wait a week or more before putting it into the water, do so. I know it will be hard to resist, but it is worth the wait to harden the finish. It takes a month or more to achieve a real hard finish. After a year, the finish is super hard. It takes just 2 cans of primer and 2-3 cans of paint to cover the hull, depending on the color. I have found that the gray primer is easier to cover in one coat than the red primer, unless the top coat color is red. Since red is such a transparent color, the red primer works better with the red paint. Red can be, as I mentioned, a difficult color to apply, but it sure makes for a sharp looking canoe when it is accented with ash. Green goes on much easier than red paint. I have not dared to try other colors, like Gloss Grape, yet. The whole painting process can be completed in less than an hour, and, aside from some finger and wrist fatigue from pressing the button on the top of the can, is a fun and rewarding process. The result is a fine, glossy hull that you can be proud of.

Where to Get Materials

Lumber: Our local Menard's store carries rough-cut 16' Western red cedar 2x4s. The 4 that I needed, however, were at the bottom of the bin, into which the lumber was very tightly stored. I had boards strewn all over the outdoor (but under cover) lumber yard while digging for the coveted clear, straight and dry boards. It is perhaps best to do such searches when the store is not busy. The cost, at the time, was about $18. 50. I ripped 3 and 1/2 of them for the needed planks.

Epoxy Resin, Fiberglass Fabric, Tape, Blended Filler and Fairing Compound: Bateau.com is a wonderful boat building web site, with many interesting plans to spend long winter hours dreaming about. My son and I built their OD 18, an 18' center console dory, and brought it Florida; where it spent 4 years at my sister's place as a boat for us to use when we visited them. Unfortunately, they moved to a condominium complex that did not allow boats, so we were forced to sell her (the boat, not my sister). Anyway, everything needed for glassing the hull can be obtained from them for a reasonable cost. I have had good luck with their economical "Marinepoxy" resin, and the 2014 price for a one and one half gallon set was $96.75. That is more than should be needed for the project, but it is best to have some extra. The blended filler is $8 for 2 ounces, which may be enough for the project, but the half pound is $25 and will be good for about 3 canoes. Five yards of 50" biaxial cloth (45/45) was $47.75, and 5 yards of 4 ounce 30" wide woven fabric was $18.75. A 24 ounce set of Quick Fair was $29.66, and may just do 2 canoes. A 50 yard roll of 3" fiberglass tape was $30; enough for a few canoes.

Nylon Seat Webbing: I can purchase 1" black nylon webbing locally for about 47 cents/foot, which is what I did for my first 2 canoes. Since then I have found 1" webbing through Amazon.com, which is double the thickness, having a tensile strength of 4200 pounds, for about 40 cents/foot. It is sold in 10 yard rolls from a company called Country Brook Design. The 10 yard roll (2014) was $11.95. Unfortunately, it takes, with my seat dimensions, just over a roll and a half to cover the seats (just under 50 feet). It is impressively strong, attractive, and easy to work with.

Brass Tubing and Stainless Steel Machine Screws: The 7/32" brass tubing, enough for 3-4 canoes, is available at Ace Hardware for about $5, as are the 3" #10 stainless steel machine screws. The 4" stainless steel screws were purchased through Fastenall, but they had to be ordered. Fortunately (for me) I was able to get a package of 50 of them, on clearance, for about $7. We can get away with using 3 and 1/2" screws on the bow seat, but I doubt they are any easier to find than the 4" screws.

Getting There

Once you have built your canoe you can do what everyone else with a canoe does; lash the craft to the top of your vehicle, head to any water body that can be driven to, and launch your canoe. Or you can take it a step farther and get your canoe to that special, secluded little lake that this craft was designed to be a part of. These small lakes can be well-guarded secrets; and for good reason. Although many times teeming with fish, they are easily over-fished if word gets out; especially if they are too easy for too many to access. Finding a few of these special lakes is half the fun. The other half is getting there.

The easiest way to obtain a canoe trailer to pull behind a bicycle, or to pull by hand, is to go on-line and order one. Some are available, complete with hitches, for about $200. But that is $200 that I would just as soon not spend, so I went ahead and designed my own trailer using free bicycle wheels and a wood/metal frame. Although it is a bit cumbersome to double-up the frame for each bicycle wheel, I could not bear to go out and buy new tires and wheels that are adapted to a single axle; not when bicycles are now-days a fairly disposable piece of equipment, and used wheels and tires are generally free for the asking at bike shops, yard sales or scrap yards. Starting with free wheels goes a long way towards whittling down the cost of a trailer.

Unfortunately it is only the front wheels that are suitable for this trailer. Two front tires of equal size- and preferably similar tread patterns- are therefore required, although not all that difficult to find. The 26" mountain bike wheels are ideal for this project. Since a bicycle axle extends less than an inch from the bearing on each side of the hub, and is designed to bolt to a fork, we need to create a frame that allows the axle to similarly attach to our trailer.

I wanted my trailer to be fairly light-weight, but strong enough to withstand the abuse that a rock, root and stump-infested footpath has to offer. I wanted to use fairly thin wood, but I worried about its strength. I used scrap cedar planks for my first side rails, and they worked fine, but I wanted a bit more reassurance that they would be strong, so I switched to 1/2" plywood.

The hitch itself was a bit of a head-scratcher, since it must flex in all directions as one goes up and down hills and around corners. Again, these hitches may be purchased, but that kind of dependence on the ingenuity of others is what makes the cost of so many projects get out-of-hand. Since it is only a 60 pound canoe being pulled a relatively short distance, I opted for a spring covering a piece of reinforced tubing, which is inserted into 3/4" conduit and pinned to a 1/2" metal thimble that slips over the seat post, as my universal joint. This is probably the place where I should print several paragraphs of illegibly small print freeing me from becoming lawyer fodder should someone be injured while pulling a canoe using my method. Without going on a rant about the need for common sense and personal responsibility, let me just say that this design works for me; but feel free to simply buy a hitch from a company that has spent the money to lawyer-proof itself. Oh, and always wear a helmet, a life jacket, steel-toed shoes, ear protection and safety glasses, and definitely do not attempt to undertake this project in the State of California.

Beside the two 26" bicycle wheels, we will need a 2'x4' piece of good quality exterior grade 1/2" plywood, about 15 feet of 3/4" metal conduit, a foot of 1" aluminum angle bracket, four 3' lengths of 1/4" threaded rod (I buy two 6' lengths and cut them in half), a stiff compression spring, a piece of reinforced air hose or fuel line, a 1/4"x2"wire lock pin, a 1/2" thimble, some #10 machine screws with nylon lock nuts, and four 1/4" nylon lock nuts. The whole rig should cost less than $30.

Start by cutting the plywood into a piece 2'x35", and from it rip 10 strips each 2" in width. Two of the strips will be used for the bunks on the trailer. Stack 8 of the strips side by side and put a pencil line across them, so the edges can be identified.

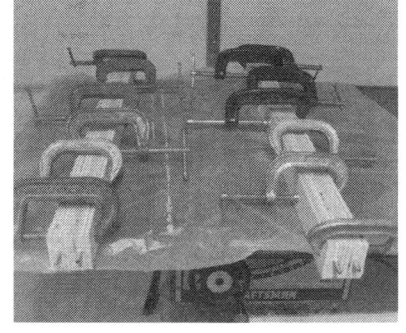

Set the table saw blade depth to 1/8" (find something 1/8" thick to use as a guide), and set the rip fence 7/8" from an inward leaning saw tooth. Run a piece of scrap wood through the saw to verify the blade depth and the distance. Then run each of the plywood strips through the saw, first with all edges having the pencil mark against the fence, turn them all and run them through again with the pencil mark away from the fence. This should create a 1/4"x1/8" deep slot which, when the 2 halves are joined together, will create a channel to hold the 3' threaded rod. Set the rods into each of four strips, with 1/2" sticking out of each end, all with the pencil marked edge the same direction. Apply a good amount of wood glue to the faces, and set the top strips on, again with the marked edges facing the same direction. Securely clamp them together, in groups of 2, with C-clamps on a plastic covered flat surface.

Cut the conduit into two 48" long pieces. Note that there should be some lines, running from end to end- left behind from the production process- that we are going to use as a guide while flattening four seats for attaching the side rails. The lines will help us to keep the flattened areas all in alignment. I have a 6" vise, which is about as small as we should go for crimping 3/4" conduit. Starting at one end, measure and mark at 1" and again at 5" and 6". Repeat on the other end. Set the pipe in the vise at the 1" mark and make a mark on the vise to line up the reference line, which will keep us from misaligning our crimps. Adjust the pipe so that the lines line up. Flatten the end, and then flatten the 1" space that is 5" from the end.

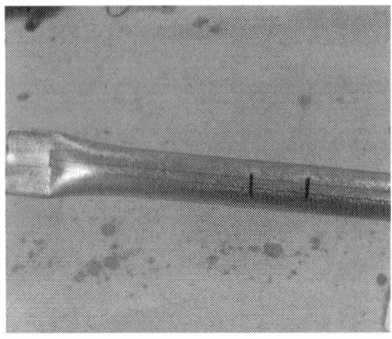  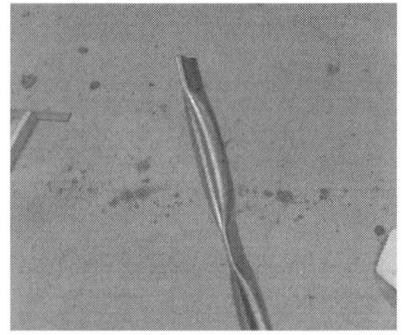

This interior crimp is a bit tricky, at least on my vise, since the shoes are not thick enough to avoid denting the pipe outside of the intended area to be flattened; but it can be done. Move the pipe to flatten the entire 1" marked area. Once flattened, mark the center of each flattened seat, and drill a 1/4" hole to receive the threaded rod ends. Repeat the process for the other pipe. I should mention that the 4" spacing between the side rails is typical for 26" mountain bike wheels. If you have wheels with axles of a different length, adjust the distance between side rails accordingly. If all of this is too confusing, the cross bars can be made from plywood, but the threaded rod end would have to be longer. A dado cut to notch out for the side rails would probably be a good idea.

The 4 side rails can now be attached to the cross bars, following a bit of sanding to get the side rails looking decent. I took it a step further, however, and ran the side rails through the router to round them off a bit; except for the bottom 3" section in the center, where the wheel brackets are to be attached. Mark the bracket locations and stop the router before crossing them, if you decide to show-off a bit and round the rail edges. I follow this up with a light sanding and a coat or 2 of spar varnish.

The four 3" long wheel brackets are made from the 1" aluminum, which was chosen for its workability. The hole for the axle is a large one (about 3/8"), but varies with axle type. The aluminum makes drilling this hole, and notching it out, much easier than it would be using steel. Two 1/4" holes are also drilled for attaching the bracket to the underside of the rails using 1/4"x1" lag screws. This attachment method may be a weak link in the building process, but, until the brackets fall off on me, I am not going to mess with bolting the brackets on by drilling through the rail. The internal threaded rod complicates this anyway. Prior to screwing the brackets on I shoot some wood glue into the pilot holes. I know it is not the proper use for wood glue, but it makes me feel better. This whole process will likely be improved upon by many who read this and say; "Why did the dumb bunny do it that way?" and I am fine with that. In fact, I do the same thing as I critique the ideas of others. Flat plate metal on the inside faces of the side rails, which are bolted through them, would likely make a better bracket. They could even be recessed inside of a shallow dado cut. I do my best, however, to balance cost, ease of construction, and availability of materials, with durability. As I have learned all too well, anything is possible if money is no object. Center one bracket and attach it to the underside of the side rail with the lag screws. Set the matching bracket on the other side rail and set the wheel into the brackets. Center the wheel between the side rails, then mark and drill pilot holes and attach the lag screws. Once the wheels are where they should be I like to insert a self-tapping screw above or below the lock nut on the threaded rod as further assurance that the side rails will not pivot. When tightening the lock nut, do not over-tighten, or the threaded rod may break (I am speaking from experience). The quarter inch rod is not very strong, although I believe it is strong enough. If in doubt, you may wish to embed 5/16" rod in the side rails.

The bunks that will support the canoe on the frame can now be installed on the cross bars. Cut 4 pieces, each 15" long, from the 2 remaining strips of plywood. Drill 3/16" holes, centered on the strips, for #10 machine screws 1" or so from the inside end and 2" from the outside end.

Mark the center of each cross bar, and drill holes to attach the wood on the pipes, after cutting 1" spacers to go under each of the outer holes. I use 3/4" plastic tubing with a bit of a saddle cut into one end with a half round file. This keeps the spacer put as it straddles the round pipe. Be sure to countersink the screw heads so they do not scratch the hull. The wood is then covered with a 2" piece of heavy tape, followed by some heavy fabric attached by stapling it to the underside of the plywood.

Cut a piece of conduit long enough to run from the back of the stem deck to the seat post on a bicycle, with a foot or so of space remaining between the stem of the canoe and the tire of the bicycle. For my set-up a 40" long piece of conduit worked well. Flatten about an inch of both ends of the conduit (they do not need to be in alignment) and then fabricate a bracket that will slip under the stem deck. I use 3/4" PVC trim board, but I imagine plywood would also work as bracket material. From it, I cut 2 blocks, each about 2 and 1/2" wide. The top block is about 1 and 1/2" long and the bottom block is about 3" long. The two are stacked as shown in the photograph, and 2 holes are drilled through the flattened conduit and both blocks. Some washers are added between the flattened conduit and the top block to widen the gap between the conduit and the bottom of the stem deck, but if the block still does not slip under it, the gap will need further widening. You may chose to simply attach a bracket of some sort to the conduit without first flattening it. These instructions are merely guidelines that leave a lot of room for improvisation. I use the 1" belt of my sander to widen the gap by removing some of the bottom block. PVC trim board is easy to cut and sand, making it a good material for this bracket.

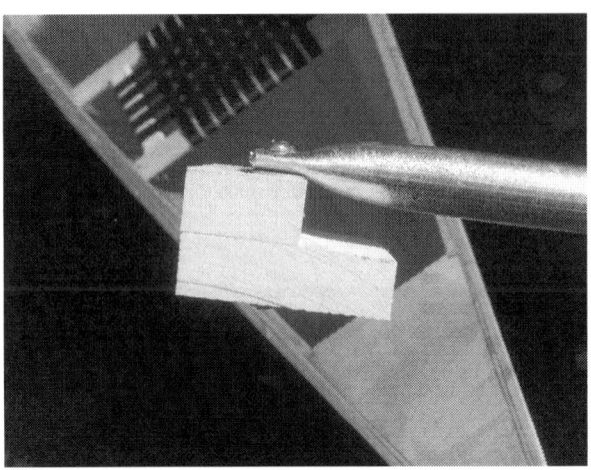 

Once the bracket fits snugly under the stem deck, mark for a 1/4" hole through the conduit over the 3/8" rope hole that had been (hopefully) previously drilled through the deck. A 1/4" carriage bolt, with the head on the underside, secures the pipe with a wing nut on the top. A piece of heavy tape on the underside of the pipe protects the deck. There is more tongue weight on the stern end due to the placement of the seats, so we attach the hitch to the stern.

Cut the pipe about 2 and 1/2 to 3" back from the flattened end that attaches to the seat post.

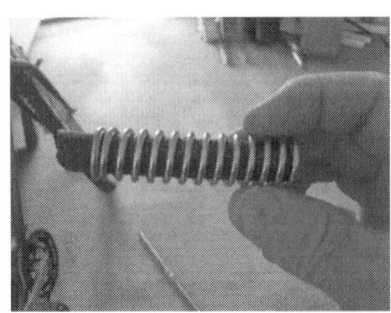
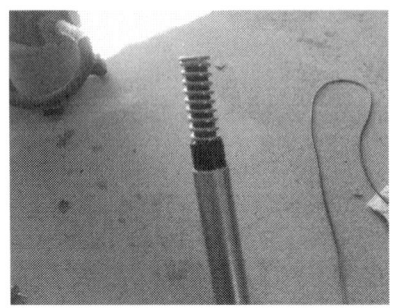
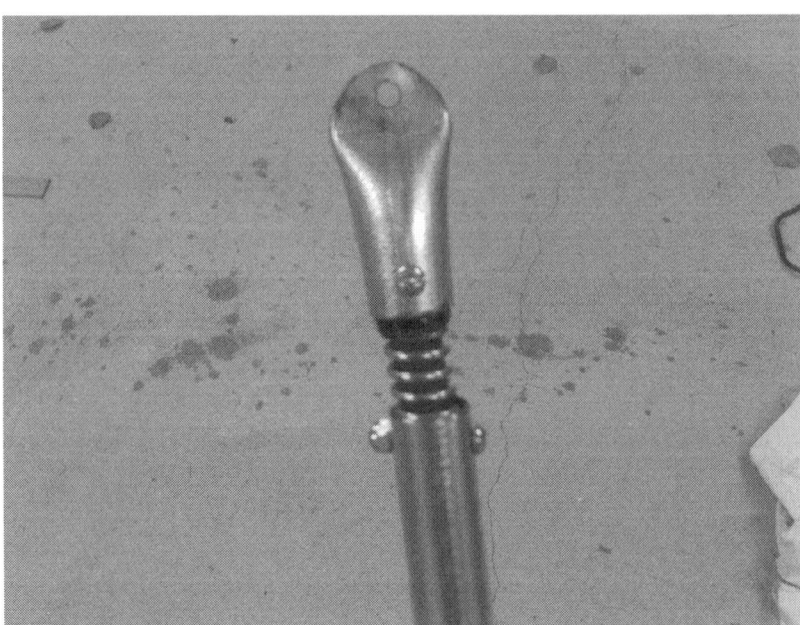

This should leave enough rounded pipe to accept an inch and a half or so of the spring and tubing; enough to securely attach it with a bolt. The spring should be as close to the end of the hitch as possible. The search for a stiff spring about 4" long and a bit more than 3/4"diameter may be a challenge. I found heavy 3/4" diameter springs easily, however, for less than $1, and wrapped some heavy duty tape around each end of the spring so it would fit snugly inside of the conduit. A piece of 1/2" air hose or fuel line is then inserted inside of the spring; it will likely need to be screwed into it.

A hole is then drilled through the conduit for a #10 machine screw to pass between the coils of the spring. The hole will be angled a bit due to the coils, which is OK. The drill bit should be allowed to be directed on its path by the coils. We do not want to force things and drill through the metal coils. Snug things up with a lock nut. The same is done on the other end of the spring, but the flattened end is to be vertical so that it will slide into the thimble.

The 1/2" thimble may need to be widened a bit to slide over the seat post, since the diameters of seat posts vary. The pointed protrusions on the ends of the thimble are lopped off with the angle grinder, and are then rounded; ideally on a disc/belt sander. A 1/4" hole is then drilled through both arms of the thimble, about 5/16" from the ends, to accept the 1/4"x2" pin. Some 1" PVC pipe or conduit is cut to slide over the seat post above and below the thimble, as a spacer. The top piece is only about 1/2" long, and the length of the bottom piece will vary, depending on the seat height. A larger diameter seat post may require slightly larger pipe. I wrapped some sand paper around a piece of 3/4" metal conduit to ream out and slightly increase the inside diameter of the plastic tubing for my seat posts.

Before pinning the hitch to the seat post it is a good idea to fashion some sort of safety strap, should the spring joint fail. I made a simple strap from scrap seat webbing, but a short section of light chain or cable would also work. Two flat straps are all that are needed to secure the canoe to the trailer once it is centered on the bunks. I find that pulling the canoe behind a bicycle is a great way to draw attention to oneself; in a good way. It is a crowning touch to a rewarding project to have passers-by slowing to make a comment, with my favorite being:

"Did you make that?"

About the Author

Mark Schultz is a Minnesota native who-after obtaining a degree in Environmental Studies from Bemidji State University-joined the Peace Corps for what was intended to be a 2 year leave-of-absence from his beloved State. Two years became 18 as he worked in freshwater aquaculture in Central Africa, Oklahoma, Florida and New York as well as in Surface Water Management with the State of Florida. The running theme throughout his career, however, has been water. He now contentedly resides in Turtle River, Minnesota with his wife and family.

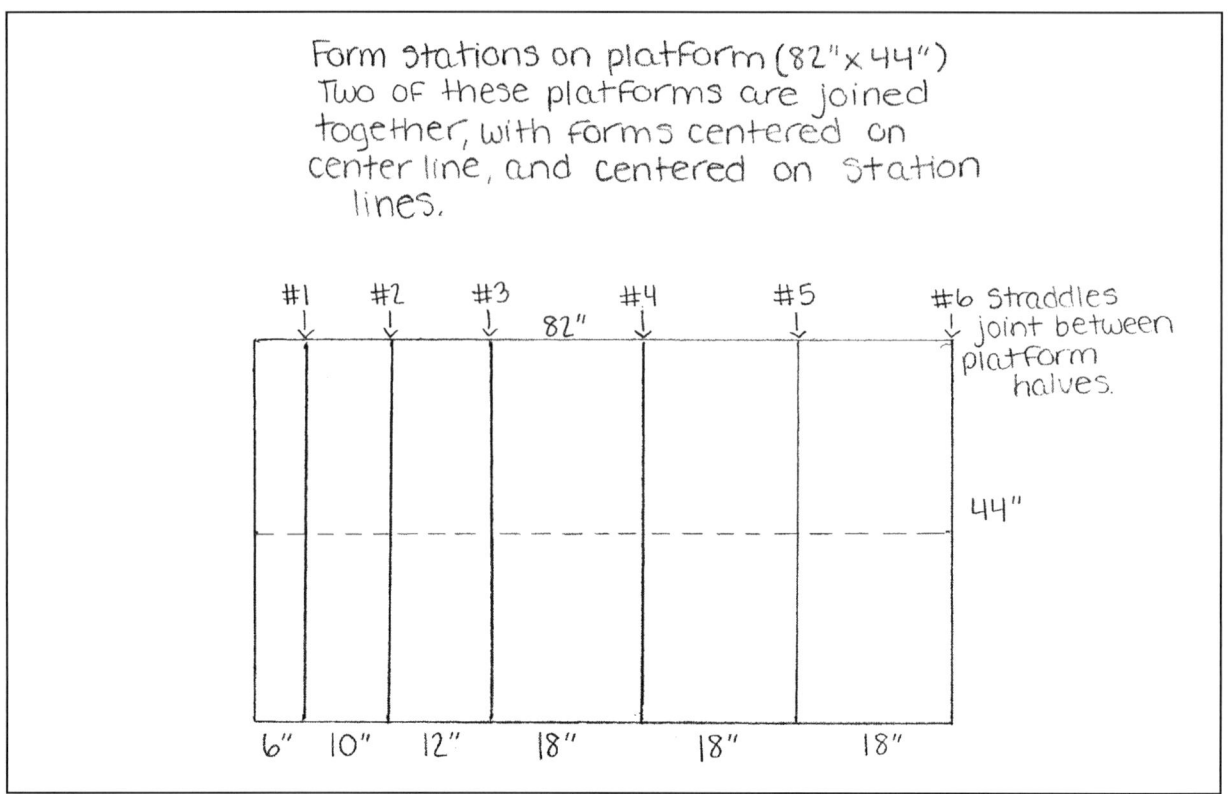

Form Platform

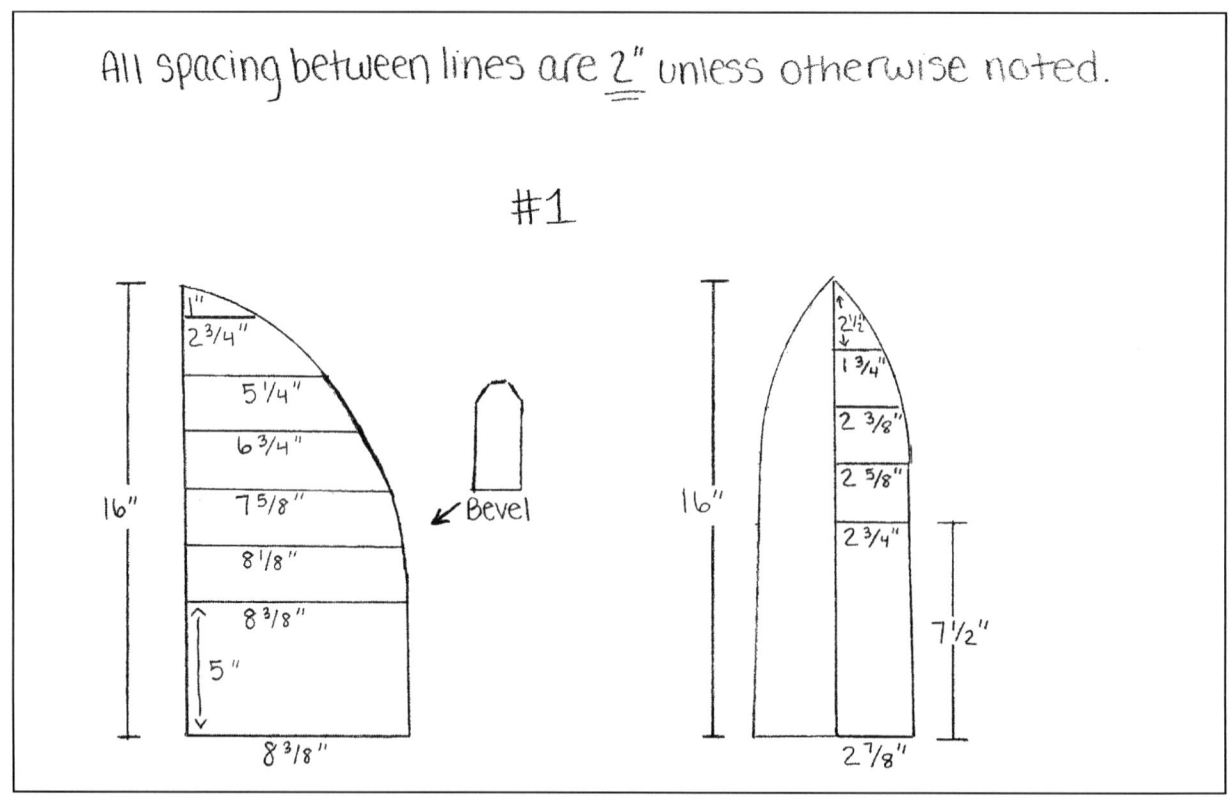

Form #1

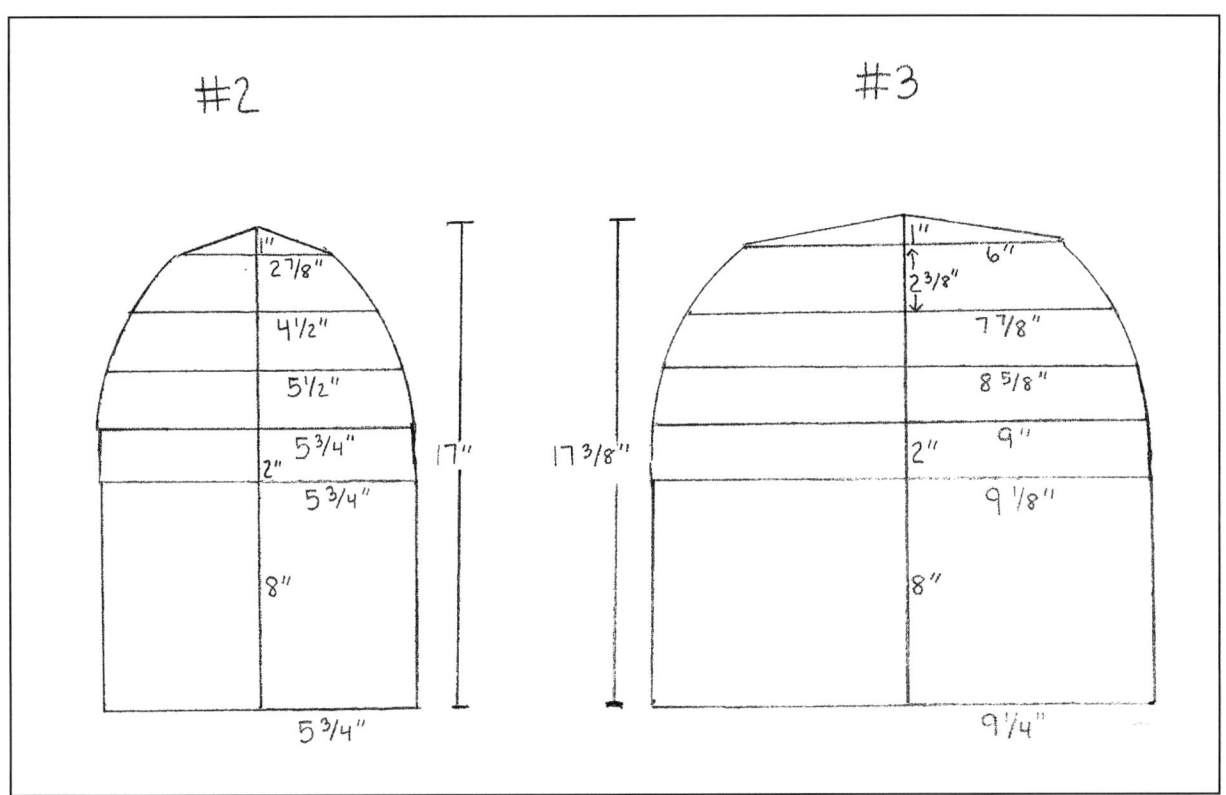

Forms #2 and #3

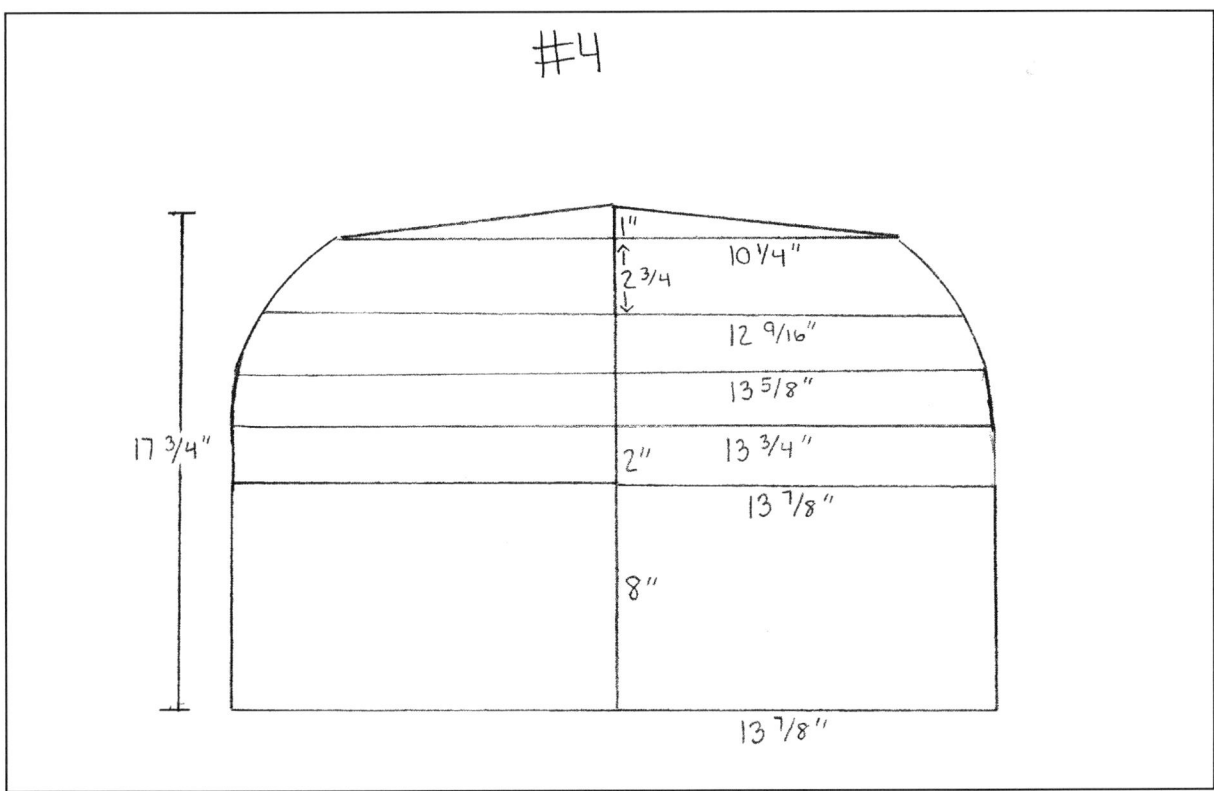

Form #4

Making a Ripple 59

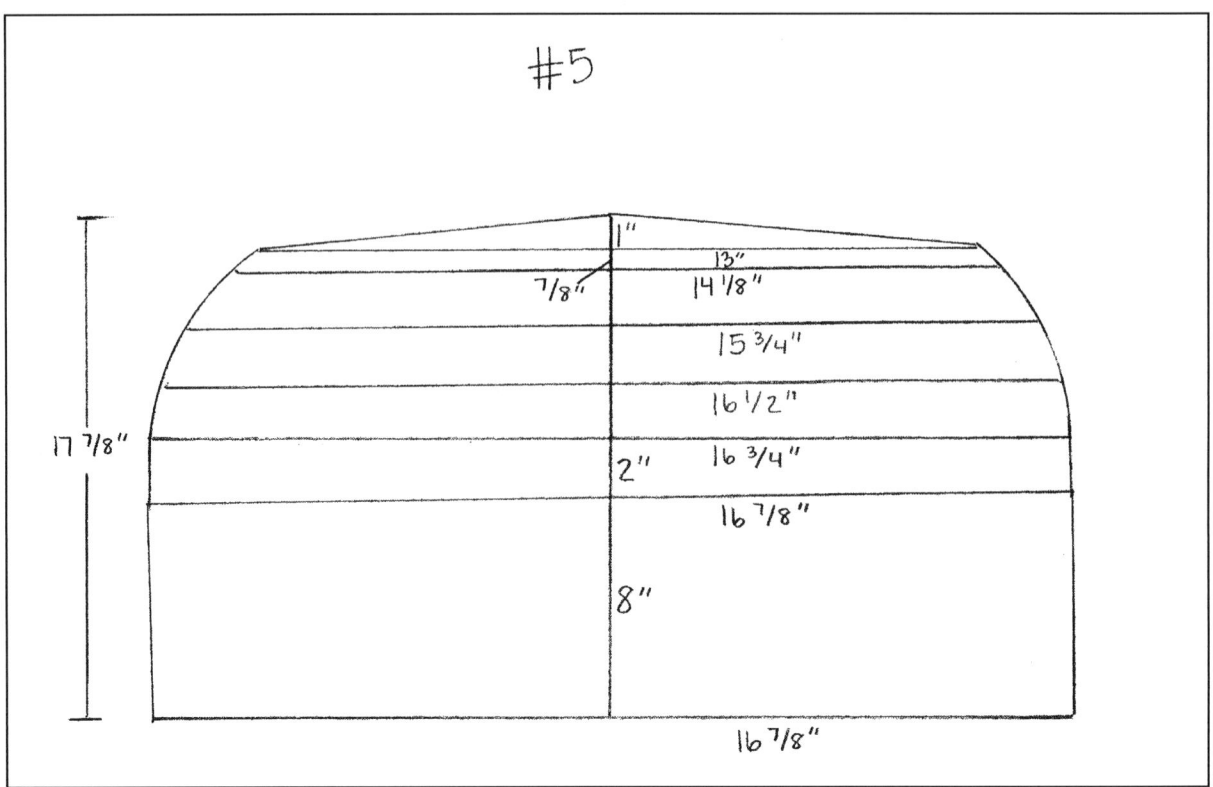

Form #5

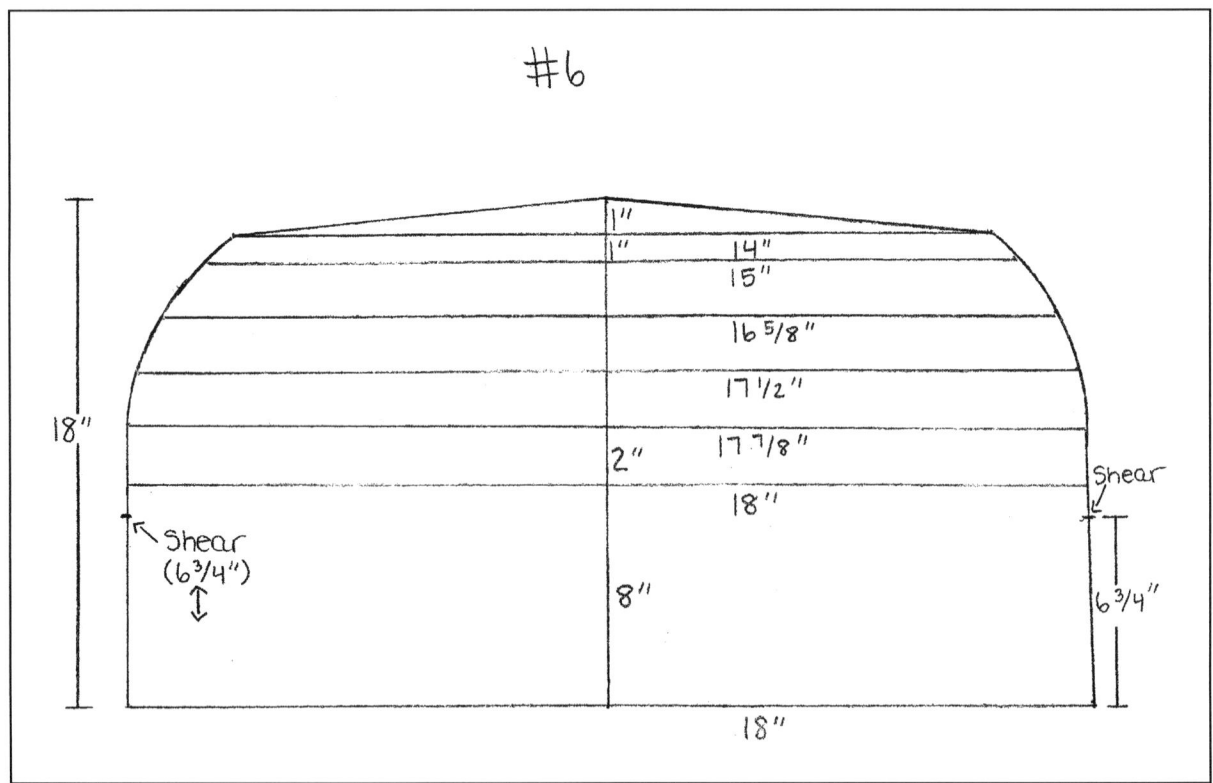

Form #6